W9-BVV-585

21

THE WRONG HORSE

THE WRONG HORSE

The Politics of Intervention and the Failure of American Diplomacy

by LAURENCE STERN

Times
BOOKS

Wingate College Library

Copyright © 1977 by Laurence Stern.
All rights reserved, including the right to reproduce this book or
portions thereof in any form. For information, address: Times
Books, a division of Quadrangle/The New York Times Book
Co., Inc., Three Park Avenue, New York, N.Y. 10016. Manufac-
tured in the United States of America. Published simultaneously
in Canada by Fitzhenry & Whiteside, Ltd., Toronto.

Book design: Beth Tondreau

Library of Congress Cataloging in Publication Data

Stern, Laurence.
 The wrong horse.

 Includes index.
  1. United States—Foreign relations—Greece.
2. Greece—Foreign relations—United States.
3. United States—Foreign relations—Turkey.
4. Turkey—Foreign relations—United States.
5. Cyprus—History—Cyprus crisis, 1963- 6. Cyprus—
History—Cyprus crisis, 1974- I. Title.
E183.8.G8S78 1977 327'.2'0973   77-6913
ISBN 0-8129-0734-5

096535

To Susan, Chris, Cathy, Gunther, Marc and Sherlock—
all of whom contributed in their own way

Contents

Acknowledgments

I would like to express my thanks to the Carnegie Endowment for International Peace which funded a year of study and travel to undertake this book, particularly to Thomas L. Hughes, president of the Carnegie Endowment; Richard Holbrooke, then editor of *Foreign Policy* magazine, as well as to Carnegie staff members Ruth Kiker, Wendy Seagrave, Fred Kirchstein, Jean Siotis, Jane Freundel and Diane Bendahmane. I am also in the debt of Benjamin Bradlee, Howard Simons, Richard Harwood and Harry Rosenfeld for indulging me my year of absence from *The Washington Post* newsroom. My gratitude also goes to John Simon of Times Books, Les Whitten, Strobe Talbot, Brian Atwood, Senator Thomas Eagleton, Jim Pyrros, Rep. John Brademas, Rep. Benjamin Rosenthal, Clifford Hackett, John Ritch, and Bill Richardson. In the ranks of the Executive Branch I made claims on the time of many, some of whom will keenly disagree with the theses of this book, among them: Henry Kissinger, Clark Clifford, Joseph Sisco, Henry Tasca, Phil Stoddard, Ambassador William Macomber, Monteagle Stearns, Tom Boyatt, Jack Maury, Lowell Citron, Nelson Ledsky, John Day, Col. George Marder, Ambassador William Crawford. Among the actors in the drama who were also kind enough to extend me their time: the late Archbishop Makarios, Rauf Denktash, George Clerides, Evangelos Averoff-Tossizza, Andros Nicolaides, Nikos Dimitriu, John Nicolopoulos, Yannis Roubatis, Tom Manthos, Hudai Yalivar. I only regret my inability to thank the many dozens more whose help is inestimable.

"So agile was Metternich's performance that it was forgotten that its basis was diplomatic skill and that it left the fundamental problems unsolved, that it was manipulation and not creation."

A World Restored, Henry A. Kissinger

THE WRONG HORSE

Introduction

The tall man with the tightly packed white curls and the impeccable double-breasted suit that was his trademark boarded a commercial flight bound for Frankfort at midday on February 15, 1977. He was accompanied on the flight from Dulles International Airport by a delegation of State Department aides bearing their bureaucratic baggage of briefing papers and memoranda.

Clark M. Clifford, now seventy years of age and a Washington lawyer of legendary influence and retainer, had just been sworn in by President Carter as his special envoy to mediate the dangerously sputtering conflict between Greece and Turkey over Cyprus. The trip signaled a new diplomatic offensive by a new American president to solve one of the knottiest and most persistent and potentially deadly problems on the American foreign policy horizon. It was a challenge worthy of Clark Clifford, whose clientele comprised the richest and most powerful interests in the American corporate world and who had been giving his counsel to presidents and foreign heads of state for thirty years. He had sat at Harry Truman's side as a White House Staff Counsel in his apprenticeship days in Washington. John Kennedy had asked him to plan the governmental transition of 1960. Lyndon Johnson sought his advice on a wide variety of personal and political problems, finally conferring on Clifford the office of Secretary of Defense—a role in which Clifford reversed the course of Johnson's Vietnam war policies.

It is unlikely that Jimmy Carter knew what a stroke of historical irony it had been to choose Clark Clifford as his mediator in the Cyprus muddle. In the Truman White House three decades earlier, Clifford had worked over the words of the speech, delivered on March 12, 1947, that was to launch the Truman Doctrine declaring Greece and Turkey to be the first clients of the postwar Western alliance to contain Soviet power. It was a speech that articulated in carefully drawn and resounding phrases America's entry into the Cold War.

For that matter, few people in Washington sensed that irony on that crisp February day when Clifford set off across the Atlantic first to Vienna to meet with U.N. Secretary-General Kurt Waldheim, and then to the parties in dispute: Greek Prime Minister Constantine Karamanlis, a skilled and pro-American politician who was nonetheless deeply vulnerable to both the right and the left on the Cyprus issue; Turkish Premier Suleyman Demirel, leader of a stalemated coalition government and himself a hostage to hard-line national sentiment on Cyprus; and finally, the late Archbishop Makarios, a brilliant practitioner of nonalignment, who had managed by deft acts of diplomatic gamesmanship to maintain the fragile reality of Cypriot national sovereignty.

The military forces of Greece and Turkey were in a state of readiness, not against the prescribed Communist enemies to the north and east, but against each other along their common Aegean and Mediterranean borders. The combustion chamber of the East Mediterranean was primed, and Cyprus could well be the spark.

Clifford's mission, as he conceived it, would be to save the alliance of which, years earlier, he had been one of the principal draftsmen. His itinerary—Athens, Ankara, and Nicosia—had been traveled by other senior diplomatic firemen dispatched from the White House. In 1964, George Ball, then Undersecretary of State for Political Affairs, was sent by President Johnson to snuff out the flames of an impending Greek-Turkish war over Cyprus. In the 1967 crisis, Cyrus Vance, then Johnson's Secretary of the Army, was sent to the same three capitals to keep NATO's house in order. In 1974, the role fell to Joseph B. Sisco, who had accompanied Ball as his chief deputy on the 1964 trip and inherited his title of Undersecretary for Political Affairs.

The past missions, which will be described in these pages, were attempts at hastily improvised "quick fixes" to patch up the growing fissures in a military alliance that had grown increasingly out of touch with the political realities of what Walter Lippmann once called the "post-postwar world." For essential to the maintenance of an alliance is a recognition by all members that their common purposes outweigh their differences.

Clifford's strategy was to convince the contending parties of their common purposes. When he sat down for consultation with Karamanlis and Demirel, he admonished that "the United States is not going to sit by idly and see developments take place which would substantially weaken NATO."

Any time two NATO allies become involved in hostilities, he told the leaders of both countries, the "NATO defense line" was weakened. He spoke of Cyprus as a "constant exacerbation" in the East Mediterranean. "Even though we have humanitarian concerns in Cyprus—the refugees and loss of lives and property—that is not our main concern. Our main concern is that Cyprus brings instability to the East Mediterranean," Clifford bluntly lectured his hosts.

Similar words had been heard before from American lips by leaders in Athens, Ankara, and Nicosia. They had been delivered in honeyed diplomatic nuance, in stern admonitions, and also in the form of dire warning. The most celebrated example of the last was President Johnson's 1964 letter to Turkish Premier Inonu ordering him to desist from a military invasion of Cyprus or face the prospect of a Soviet reaction without American help. Earlier that year, in Nicosia, Ball berated a silent and unyielding Makarios and accused him of turning "this beautiful little island into your private *abattoir*." Ball returned to Washington empty-handed.

"Why do you Americans care so much about Cyprus?" Clifford was asked by his Turkish government hosts during the February consultations. The American lawyer pondered the question and then replied that the U.S. Congress had found Turkey to be in violation of the laws against using American weapons for aggressive purposes, in this instance in Cyprus. Congress is not going to change its mind unless you take substantial steps in Cyprus, he told the Turks. "Congress says, why should we do something for Turkey until Turkey does something about Cyprus?" Then Clifford parried the question.

"Why does Turkey care so much about Cyprus?" he asked his confounded hosts.

The complexities and contradictions of the Turkish aid debate in Congress, with its mix of partisan politics, foreign policy dispute, ethnic lobbying, and moral and legal argumentation, sowed anger and confusion in Ankara. Kissinger had earlier portrayed the issue in simpler terms: the military aid cutoff to Turkey was engineered by the Greek lobby and by the administration's opponents in Congress. What was the point of an alliance, the Turks asked aloud, when the supply of needed weapons to Turkey became hostage to the demands of a Greek lobby? But there was also the question of what logic there was to an alliance in which two important members were preoccupied with arming for war with each other.

Clifford's sense of frustration with what appeared to him as the irrationality of the Greeks and Turks was understandable. Overriding logic with emotions in the Cyprus dispute were centuries of conflict the depth of which no State Department briefing paper could convey. And of all the emissaries sent from Washington, Clifford, though the most experienced in negotiation, was the most innocent in the history of those ancient enmities.

This book will examine some of the background of the conflict from an American perspective. Since World War II, the United States has had a growing influence in the events that contributed to the present explosive muddle in the East Mediterranean. By the time Clifford arrived on the scene as the latest in a procession of special U.S. envoys, Cyprus was not only a term of geographical reference. It had become a metaphor for American foreign policy failure under the leadership of Secretary of State Henry Kissinger. Kissinger had himself been quoted as admitting that Cyprus took him unaware, more so than any other crisis in his eight years as chief architect of American foreign policy.

The past American failure, as Clifford would privately acknowledge, transcended the actions of the United States during the midsummer coup in 1974 against Makarios. It was rooted in the steadily warming embrace during the Nixon years of the military regime that had seized power in Athens on April 21, 1967, and ended democratic and constitutional government for seven years. In the eyes of Nixon and Kissinger, the military regime was the horse to bet on to ensure Greece's adherence to the military-political goals of NATO, a decision that was engraved in National Security Council scripture within a year after Nixon took office. Yet from 1970 onward, the colonels in Athens organized and supported conspiracies against Archbishop Makarios and the national sovereignty of Cyprus. These are detailed in the following pages.

During the period of military rule in Greece, the United States pursued a dual foreign policy: It paid public lip service to the objective of restoring constitutional government in Athens while supporting with arms, money, and gestures of approval a regime that could not survive the reestablishment of democracy. Greece's most prominent civilian leaders, from conservative to radical, were in jail, in exile, or simply silent. American diplomats in Athens were under orders to pay them no attention.

Greece was safe for NATO. But its political condition seemed to mock the resounding phrases uttered by Harry Truman on March 12, 1947, words that Clark Clifford helped to polish. It was the Truman Doctrine speech that proclaimed Greece and Turkey as the first beneficiaries of a new American postwar policy to sow the world with American aid —arms, money, and military commitments—to keep the Soviet dragon at bay.

"At the present moment in world history nearly every nation must choose between alternative ways of life," Truman said.

> One way of life is based upon the will of the majority, and is distinguished by free institutions, representative government, free elections, guarantees of individual liberty, freedom of speech and religion, and freedom from political oppression.
>
> The second way of life is based upon the will of the minority forcibly imposed on the majority. It relies upon terror and oppression, a controlled press and radio, fixed elections and the suppression of personal freedoms.

Greece had chosen the former. Yet for seven years, with the active cooperation of the United States, it had to endure the latter way of life. When democracy returned to Athens with the collapse of the military regime in July 1974, no thanks were owed to the Americans for the deliverance. America had put its political bets on the wrong horse.

President Carter, Secretary of State Vance, and Special Envoy Clifford are still on the foothills of a diplomatic trail that is littered with the bones of false hopes, broken promises, and flawed assumptions of the past. One of the most important keys to an understanding of the Cyprus muddle is the realization that the United States, far from being a disinterested broker to the disputes of the past, was a deeply involved participant. The purpose of this book is to examine some aspects of that involvement.

PART I

1. The Foreign Factor

At about five o'clock on the morning of April 21, 1967, the United States CIA Station Chief in Athens, John M. Maury, was awakened by the screeching of the emergency radio in his second-floor study which served as a direct link with the American embassy communications center. He learned, as he later recounted in writing, that "the military controlled Athens, all communications had been cut and all movement on the streets forbidden. Combat-equipped troops controlled every radio transmitter, airport, railway station, telephone central, power plant, police station and intersection."

Maury jumped into his clothes and headed for the embassy in his chauffeur-driven Cadillac. Main boulevards were choked with tanks moving toward the center of the city. In the Ambelokipi district, Maury's car was stopped and the American CIA Station Chief was informed by a Greek soldier that he would be permitted to go no further. Maury noticed, however, that the American military attaché and other senior U.S. officers in uniform were being waved through the roadblocks, with smart salutes from the Greek troopers. So the CIA official rushed home and pulled on his World War II marine uniform, seams yielding to postwar weight gains, and once again started for the roadblock. This time he, too, was passed through with a salute.

In embassy circles, Maury was admired for his patrician good manners and professional imperturbability. He was descended from an old and socially prominent Virginia family, one of whose members had for several years owned Thomas Jefferson's estate, Monticello.

Jack Maury blended perfectly into the CIA's tweedy, suede-shoe elite that had traditionally gravitated to the upper social and professional ranks of the agency. Like most of his peers in the agency, he was a man of polished style but he was not an intellectual. He was a true believer in the institutional anticommunism of the CIA. Maury was also a skilled and experienced intelligence operative who had come to Greece in 1962 from a background in Soviet affairs. Many times since arriving in Athens he had had occasion to reflect ironically upon the promise made by his boss, then Deputy Director Richard M. Helms. The Greek assignment, said Helms, would be a picnic—a vacation—after the rigors of his earlier work. During Maury's six-year tenure in Greece, there were eleven changes of Government by decree or coup.

When Maury arrived at the embassy that morning in his worn marine uniform, the customary aplomb was gone. His consternation as he rushed into the building was well remembered by others present.

"Jack Maury gave every appearance of being as much in the dark as I was that Friday morning," recalled one foreign service officer who had blustered his way, in fluent Greek, through the same roadblock. "But those committed to a conspiracy view of history," he added, "would argue that, of course, the head of the CIA station would have to give the appearance of knowing nothing and having slept through it all."

According to strict rules of historical evidence, Maury's behavior and attitude on the morning of the coup could be considered as having no more than circumstantial bearing on the question of the CIA's complicity in the affair. Indeed, in the embassy, even among those who were deeply suspicious of the agency's dealings with its Greek military intelligence counterpart, no one questioned Maury's insistence that he had no foreknowledge of the coup and that no one in the CIA station had either been aware of or taken part in its preparation. These facts are of some significance in the history and political demonology of the "revolution" of April 21, staged by the group of military intelligence officers headed by Colonel George Papadopoulos, which seized power in Greece in 1967 and maintained it until 1974.

It has been a commonly held assumption, both inside and outside Greece, that the CIA was the author, if not the chief accomplice, of the 1967 coup. For one thing, the takeover followed the lines of a NATO contingency plan, code-named Prometheus, designed to impose internal order and eliminate "subversive" leftist opposition in the event of a war with any of Greece's neighbors to the north: Bulgaria, Albania, or Yugoslavia. Moreover, this assumption of direct American involvement through activities of the U.S. intelligence service reflects the abiding Greek sense, inculcated by history and character, of a Foreign Factor—an outside influence over the country's internal affairs. The Foreign Factor, like the Eumenides of classical Greek drama, was an external force of fate that controlled the life of the Hellenic state, ancient and modern, and drove its people now toward national greatness, now toward disaster. So, at least, it was felt.

A few hours of political conversation in Athens will quickly register on a visiting American the sense of shadowy ubiquity with which the CIA haunts the Greek political consciousness. It is all too easy for outsiders to scoff at this as paranoia. But three decades of post-World War II history left the Greeks with a deeply embedded sense of manipulation by agencies of foreign influence. The Greek intelligence agency, known by the acronym KYP, was established under the direction of the CIA, and the personnel and functions of the two intelligence bureaucracies were closely intermingled.

The royal family was an important client of the American CIA. Queen Frederika and King Paul, as well as the Crown Prince and later King Constantine, maintained warm personal relations with top CIA officials. Former CIA Director Allen Dulles had been a sailing guest of the royal family and, during visits to the United States, King Paul and Queen Frederika had been house guests of John McCone, who had succeeded Dulles as CIA Director. Frederika, a woman of scathing bluntness, once remarked in the presence of a high-ranking U.S. intelligence official: "The diplomats are fairies and half-wits." She preferred to channel her business through the CIA station in Athens. The agency's services to Frederika included such varied benefactions as providing political briefings for her frequent trips abroad, working out itineraries and, in at least one case, obtaining a rare-model tape recorder that was being sought for the palace.

During George Allen's term as ambassador to Greece, he visited Dulles's Washington office to complain about the CIA's continued practice of playing Santa Claus to the palace. "I thought we were doing away with the Christmas list," Allen remonstrated, according to another senior diplomat who witnessed the unusual exchange. Dulles

Wingate College Library

shrugged with contrite surprise and turned to his Deputy for Operations, Frank Wisner. "Frank, haven't we turned this thing off?" Wisner nodded negatively, the observer recalled. "I couldn't believe what I was hearing," said the senior diplomat, now retired.

George Allen's peeve was understandable. In Athens, as in other capitals, the CIA could dip into the bottomless treasury of unvouchered funds to ingratiate itself with governing elites. Airplanes, sports cars, tape recorders, and cash were available through the unvouchered accounting system of the agency. By contrast, the State Department functioned with limited representational funds and the specter of government and congressional auditors looking over its shoulders.

According to one former political officer in the Athens embassy,

> Our intelligence people were solidly entrenched with the group in power and worked hand-in-glove with them through extensive and fairly open liaison arrangements as well as more private deals. They ignored the outs except to try to penetrate the organizations of the extreme left, subvert them, factionalize them, expose them, or otherwise disrupt their capabilities.
>
> The CIA was in bed with the palace, the army, the Greek intelligence service, the rightist parties, the conservative business community, the establishment in general.

The relationship between the palace and the U.S. intelligence service was but one example of the service's penetration of the Greek governing hierarchy during the aftermath of World War II. Greece, more than any other country in Europe, had become an American Cold War protectorate.

The process had begun with the enunciation of the Truman Doctrine. At that time, the United States had formally assumed from Britain the role of Greece's chief protector and along with it a national commitment: to support Greece and Turkey as the southern bulwark of the then emerging anti-Communist alliance of Western Europe, the North Atlantic Treaty Organization.

In setting forth his request to the joint session of Congress for a grant of $400 million to Greece and Turkey, President Truman had raised the specter of a Communist takeover:

> The very existence of the Greek state is today threatened by the terrorist activities of several thousand men, led by Communists,

who defy the Government's authority at a number of points, particularly along the northern boundaries. . . . The disappearance of
Greece as an independent state would have a profound effect upon
those countries in Eastern Europe whose people are struggling
against great difficulties to maintain their freedom and independence while they repair the damages of war.

One minor paradox of history was that the insurgent Communist
forces in the Greek civil war had been led by many of the same underground figures who had formed the core of the World War II anti-
Nazi resistance in Greece. Ironically, the forces supporting the royalist
government against the Communists in the early postwar period were
made up, in significant numbers, of security forces who had collaborated with the Nazi occupation authorities.

The Senate Foreign Relations Committee met in executive session
to consider the Truman request, and there was one exchange between
then Chairman Arthur Vandenburg and Secretary of the Navy James
Forrestal that reverberates today with ironic relevance.

Vandenburg observed with all due respect that "the chief weakness
in the President's message [was] that at no point did he bring this
hazard home to the United States as an American hazard in any respect. He left it rather in the ideological field, of interest in freedom.

"Does not this come back to the United States and its own intelligent self-interest in a very realistic fashion?"

Secretary Forrestal replied, "Absolutely."

Vandenburg then asked, "How can you prove that to the American
people? What can you say to them? What dare you say to them on that
subject?"

At this point, the transcript, which was released more than a quarter
of a century later by the Foreign Relations Committee as part of its
historical series, carries the notation: "(*Discussion was off the record.*)"

Twenty-seven years after the fact, the executive branch still refused to declassify the Truman administration's justification for em-
barking on the massive program of Greek-Turkish aid in terms of the
"intelligent self-interest" of the American people. What failed to
emerge at the hearings or in the general public awareness was that the
government of Greece, whose call Truman had said he was heeding,
played an insignificant role in the formulation of the aid request,
which was being presented to Congress as the alternative to the Com-

munist conquest of Athens. The request had been conceived and transmitted by the newly arrived American technicians in the U.S. economic mission and embassy.

In the ensuing period, the American embassy, together with the military mission and the CIA station, had become as influential in the governing of Greece as any of the country's own political institutions. The American presence was pervasive in the cabinets, ministries, political centers, general staffs, and intelligence agencies of succeeding Greek governments.

In the immediate postwar years, the United States encouraged in Greece, as it did elsewhere in Europe, the emergence of liberal center parties built along social-democratic lines. The effort was to support these new movements as anti-Communist showcases with an emphasis on reformist social policies as a contrast to the bleak Stalinist regimes in the communized states of Eastern Europe apportioned to the Soviet sphere at Yalta and Tehran.

But by 1952, with the Cold War now at its height, the American policy line had hardened and, in Greece particularly, the U.S. embassy had become the operating center where the political interests of the Americans, the palace, the military, and the conservative parties were merged into a common front. That front was the Greek Rally party.

U.S. Ambassador John Peurifoy, an energetic cold-warrior and interventionist, was the ideal instrument to carry out these policies. To the Greek government and the palace, Peurifoy was the personification of the cornucopia of American dollars, equipment, and advisers flooding Greece in those years. He showed no hesitancy in meddling in Greek electoral procedure or in the appointment of heads of government or in other acts of high executive power. He functioned more as a prime minister than an ambassador.

One of Peurifoy's most celebrated acts of public intervention was his issuance to the Greek press in March 1952 of a warning that unless an American-favored electoral system was used in the coming November elections, there would be "destructive results upon the effective utilization of American aid to Greece." Peurifoy was waving the big stick of the aid program to exact the desired political results from Athens.

Peurifoy's act of intervention was condemned roundly in the Greek press and in the Center and Left parties as a serious intrusion into internal Greek affairs. Undaunted, the ambassador issued another declaration: "I think that the Greek public must be assured, and will believe very soon when it observes the development of events, that I am working for the benefit of Greece." The newspaper *Eleftheria* complained in its editorial that Peurifoy had assumed the role of "Governor General" of Greece. "In the name of what logic," the editorial went on, "can a military alliance, which aspires to the fortification of the independence of nations, remove from its members even their political rights?" The government itself issued a communiqué noting stiffly that "it belongs to the Greek people and government to decide with what election system the country will be administered."

Nonetheless, the Center party government of Nicholas Plasteras agreed to heed Peurifoy's admonition in behalf of the American-favored, single-member-district electoral system. In the election on November 16, 1952, the American-favored candidate, Marshal Alexander Papagos, and his newly formed Rally Party won with 49.2 percent of the popular vote; but thanks to the electoral method adopted by Plasteras, Papagos's party claimed 82.3 percent of the seats in Parliament. The election ushered in a period of conservative rule that lasted eleven years.

When Papagos died three years after the election, Peurifoy counseled King Paul to choose as his successor Constantine Karamanlis, bypassing senior leaders of the Greek Rally party such as Foreign Minister Stephanos Stephanopoulos and Panayiotis Kanellopoulos. Karamanlis was a figure of minor political importance, but he had won the admiration of the American embassy for the efficiency with which he built highways and administered American aid programs in his role as Minister of Public Works. Papagos himself had designated Stephanopoulos as his successor. The King, however, knew that the Americans were crucial to the survival of the monarchy and were also the chief providers of the Greek army, which was, in turn, the bulwark of the crown. And so, in 1955, Karamanlis assumed the prime ministership, bringing Greece eight more years of conservative and authoritarian rule.

During the period of strong American patronage stemming from Greece's strategic role as a logistical base for military and intelligence operations in the East Mediterranean, the Hellenic armed forces flourished as an almost autonomous power base. The military was nourished by some $3 billion in American money, equipment, and training. The accretion of independent power to the Greek armed services became one of the most politically important facts of life in the country's postwar history. It also reflected the pattern and priorities of American investment in Greece. It shaped the framework within which the coup of the colonels took place on April 21, 1967.

The other institution of state control that was fostered by the American presence was the KYP, the Greek Central Intelligence Service, which was funded, organized, and advised by the American CIA in the postwar years. Relations between the two sister intelligence organizations and their personnel continued to be exceedingly close. Unlike its foreign parent, the KYP combined foreign and domestic intelligence functions, and it also served as the core of the conspiracy through which the colonels assumed control of the Greek state from the throne and the senior officers of the military. It was the back-room military intelligence bureaucrats rather than the leaders of the Greek armed forces who carried out the April 1967 coup.

Now let us return to the scene in the American embassy on the morning of the April 21, 1967, coup.

If the U.S. diplomatic establishment in Athens had been directly involved in the events of April 21, then all the principal actors conspired in one of the most remarkable bureaucratic charades in diplomatic history. The first American official to learn of the coup, official records indicated, was Ambassador Phillips Talbot, who had been roused from sleep sometime after 2:00 A.M. by a visit from the nephew of Prime Minister Panayiotis Kanellopoulos. Soldiers had come, the young man reported to the ambassador, to take his uncle away "for his own protection." Would the ambassador please come, he pleaded, to assure his hysterical aunt of the Prime Minister's safety? Talbot's caller also reported that army tanks were assembling in Constitution Square, which borders the Parliament building in the center of Athens.

On his way to the Prime Minister's residence, Talbot stopped at the American chancery and sent a flash cable to Washington. He dictated the message to a code clerk who, in the haste and confusion of the moment, transmitted it as one sentence: "PRIME MINISTER KANELLOPOULOS ARRESTED BY SOLDIERS AND TANKS IN CONSTITUTION SQUARE. TALBOT."

In Washington, the watch officer phoned Greek Country Director Dan Brewster, who was perplexed by the elderly Prime Minister's being taken into custody by an armored force—not to mention what Kanellopoulos might be doing in Constitution Square in the middle of the night. And so, before returning to the State Department, Brewster dictated a skeptical reply to Athens in the name of the Secretary of State: "WHO SENT EMBTEL? WHERE IS AMBASSADOR TALBOT? RUSK."

Talbot, upon returning to the chancery and unaware of the garbled transmission of his cable, indignantly responded: "I SENT EMBTEL. I AM IN MY EMBASSY. TALBOT."

In Athens, the radio blared martial music, interrupted by occasional announcements from the new rulers of Greece. The American Armed Forces Radio station, in a supreme gesture of neutrality during the colonels' seizure of power, blared rock-and-roll music throughout the day. Talbot and the senior embassy officials, initially in a state of shock, embarked on the task of trying to assemble the facts and report them to Washington. Maury and the CIA station also scrambled for information, and within two days the American diplomats and the spies, working together within the embassy, had pieced together the basic components of the story. The most embarrassing revelation was that the American embassy, which had, in fact, been passively monitoring a prospective coup for weeks, simply had its sights trained on the wrong set of political players. The conventional wisdom within the American intelligence community in Athens was that a coup had been chartered by King Constantine and was to be executed by General Gregory Spandidakis, the Chief of the National Defense General Staff, to forestall a return to power by Center Union party leader George Papandreou and his son, Andreas. The Papandreous were by then anathema to the Greek military establishment, the palace, and a good number of the senior American diplomatic and intelligence officials.

The confusion in the American embassy was mirrored in the Greek military command structure. Top-ranking generals who were aware of the NATO contingency plan assumed that the coup was being launched with the authorization of the palace. They had no inkling that it was in fact being carried out by a band of well-organized military conspirators. If the generals had known the truth, the Papadopoulos coup would undoubtedly have sputtered out ineffectually after the first few hours.

2. The Unrelenting Struggle

The Papandreous, father and son, were the chief catalysts of changing political attitudes during the early 1960s. Both represented the leftward swing of Greek electoral opinion, and their policies were regarded as antimilitary by the army, antiroyalist by the throne, anti-NATO and anti-American by the American embassy.

George Papandreou (père) was one of Greece's most eminent political personalities, a spellbinding speaker, a man of independent judgment and behavior, and also a leader whose anti-Communist credentials were well established throughout his long public career. He headed Greece's government-in-exile in Cairo during World War II and became the country's reconstruction Prime Minister in 1944. By 1963, he had come to personify the mainstream of democratic liberalism in postwar Greek politics. As a young man, his son Andreas had become involved in left-wing politics during the prewar years. He was arrested and is believed to have been tortured when the police of the Metaxas dictatorship found evidence of his political activity. He left for the United States and spent twenty years there, studying at Harvard and then teaching economics in universities in the Midwest and California. He worked in the campaigns of Adlai Stevenson and remained actively involved in the liberal wing of the Democratic party.

In 1961, as large segments of the Greek population were beginning to bristle at the restraints of conservative rule under the premierships of Papagos and Karamanlis, the elder Papandreou formed the Center Union party. The new political movement consolidated the various center and center-left constituencies, which had been effectively fragmented during the 1950s. In the same year, Karamanlis forced an election test of his policies. The campaign reverberated with charges of fraud, terrorism, and paramilitary tactics conducted in behalf of the incumbent government. Before the campaign got under way, Constantine, who had succeeded to the throne, tried to persuade the elder Papandreou in a face-to-face meeting to endorse an election system designed to prevent Communist deputies from being elected to Parliament.

Subsequently, the CIA Station Chief in Athens, Laughlin Campbell, got into the act. Campbell's intercession led to the first major brush between the CIA and Andreas Papandreou. As recounted by Andreas,* he was invited alone to a meeting with Campbell early in the winter of 1961. The CIA official pressed Andreas for a chance to meet with his father so that he could make the case directly for the election-law change, which the palace, the Americans, and the Karamanlis camp wanted adopted. The measure, called the "kindred party system" and modeled on a French municipal election system, was a formula for the outright disenfranchisement of the Communists in parliamentary elections. It would have set up two classes of parties— one running the gamut from the conservative Rally party to the Center Union party of the Papandreous, the so-called national parties; the other including only the Communists and closely allied forces, the "nonnational" parties. Under the system, the coalition with the largest number of votes would share the seats of a particular district to the exclusion of the losing coalition. Since the Communists were unlikely to win a majority in any district, the practical effect of the kindred party system would be to confirm control for the incumbent Karamanlis government and to salvage a minority position for the Center and Center Union parties. The scheme would also preclude the election of Communists to Parliament.

Andreas told Campbell that he doubted his father would be interested in such a proposal. "If you ask him to accept the kindred party

---

*Andreas Papandreou, *Democracy at Gunpoint: The Greek Front.* Garden City, N.Y.: Doubleday, 1970, p. 108.

system, you are sure to get an immediate, negative reply. He is not about to commit political suicide to please you," Papandreou recounted as his reply to Campbell. "Campbell suddenly changed," Andreas reported. "He stood up. He spoke angrily, 'Go tell your father that in Greece we get our way. We can do what we want—and we stop at nothing.' "* (During a trip to Washington the following Christmas, Andreas protested Campbell's behavior to Carl Kaysen, a fellow economist from Harvard who had become an important staff member of the Kennedy White House. Not long afterward, Campbell was transferred out of Greece, although a direct relationship between the two events has not been confirmed.)

CIA officials have their own version of the agency's relations with Andreas. They say that after Andreas's return to Greece in 1959, he sought support from the agency and, after some deliberation, was turned down. "In those days, the CIA was interested in young people not only as intelligence sources but with political potential and influence as well," one intelligence official related. "Andreas made an interesting proposition for support, but we decided that he was too unstable—that we could not work with him."

Nonetheless, one authoritative CIA source acknowledged that the CIA did fund other Center Union political figures who provided valuable information or were generally pro-American in their views. "Without going into specific names, I would say that the identity of some of these people would surprise you very much," said the source. "They were extremely helpful in getting access to people and organizations we could not reach on our own, and they could not afford to be given overt American support." The Papandreous, according to this official, were not on the list.

The outcome of the election was another majority for Karamanlis, despite the widely publicized charges of election irregularity.

George Papandreou resolved to continue his challenge to Karamanlis and launched what he called an "unrelenting struggle" for a new election that would cancel the outcome of the 1961 presidential election and achieve the reformist policies of the Center Union movement. Papandreou decried what he called an "electoral *coup d'état*" by Karamanlis and the Right in the 1961 election. He also called for a more independent policy in foreign affairs, a neutralized Balkan zone

*Papandreou, *op. cit.*, p. 108.

stripped of nuclear bases. This message was more palatable to the moderates because of the decline in the perceived threat from the Soviet Union and its Balkan satellites. His attack provoked U.S. Ambassador Ellis Briggs to criticize the Papandreous openly and to describe the 1961 election as a model of fairness.

Then, on June 11, 1963, a sudden and dramatic development upset the political status quo. Karamanlis, a strong-willed executive leader who has been compared by some American Greece-watchers to Lyndon B. Johnson, resigned because of increasing disagreements with King Paul. The event that triggered his resignation was a planned state visit by the King to Britain, where feelings were running high against alleged political repression in Greece. There was the possibility that embarrassing demonstrations would take place. King Paul and Queen Frederika disregarded the advice of Karamanlis against going. In the background, however, was the growing political dissension in Greece, exacerbated in part by the "unrelenting struggle" of Papandreou. The Lambrakis affair, the murder of popular left-wing Deputy George Lambrakis by right-wing political goons, had become a *cause célèbre* and provided the script for the movie *Z*.

In this impasse, the American embassy favored reconstitution of the political leadership in Athens with a coalition of conservative liberals and liberal conservatives.

The King appointed a caretaker government to pave the way for new elections on November 3, 1963. Although it resulted in a marginal victory for Papandreou, it was one that made him dependent on a handful of Communist votes to achieve effective parliamentary majorities. Papandreou, who had no use for the Communists, declined to rule if he had to rely on the support of the Communist deputies. He did form a government that he led for forty-five days before resigning to bring on new elections and, he hoped, a broader governing majority. On February 16, 1964, George Papandreou won a 52.7 percent majority and carried 173 parliamentary seats out of 300. The "unrelenting struggle" seemed vindicated.

Andreas Papandreou played a role in his father's government that has been compared to the one Robert Kennedy performed in his brother's administration in Washington. From his earlier position as an economic adviser, Andreas's duties were expanded to that of a super troubleshooter and coordinator. One of the first problem areas into which he delved was the KYP, the Greek Central Intelligence

Service, and its relations with its American counterpart. He assumed the role of liaison between the two organizations. But because of the Campbell incident and the suspicions of both Papandreous concerning the role of the American CIA in the 1961 elections, relations were already strained between the two parties.

Shortly after the first victory of George Papandreou in November 1963, Maury sought to mend the ragged relationship with the Papandreous by arranging a dinner party. Wives were present, and the CIA official·tried to bring the full force of personal charm and professional wile to bear on the Papandreous. According to witnesses, Maury tried to persuade Papandreou the elder that the widely heard allegations that the CIA was working against him and his party were false. "Our job is to work with the established government and its local intelligence services," Maury is reported to have told them. The CIA, he went on, wanted to continue its relations with KYP in projects of "common interest." Yet, afterward, there was to come more evidence, in the Papandreous' eyes at any rate, that they and their party's top officials were under joint KYP-CIA surveillance. Maury's protestations that there was no CIA complicity in KYP's domestic political surveillance activities fell on skeptical ears in Athens.

"We made many efforts to get in touch with Andreas on matters of common interest," a former U.S. intelligence operative recalled. "But it was hard to get access to him. The trouble was that he was naive and deeply suspicious of U.S. motives because we had been so closely associated with Karamanlis. As a Greek, he could not believe our involvements were nonpartisan. He assumed our role was to hurt the Center Union and help Karamanlis. The people around Andreas kept his suspicions alive." Then Andreas, convinced that his own and his father's telephones were being tapped by the KYP and/or the CIA, finally set up his own intelligence service and began to place CIA officials under surveillance. Such behavior was incomprehensible to some American officials.

3. The Andreas Fixation

Andreas Papandreou became an overpowering obsession of American foreign policy managers in Athens and Washington, very much as Makarios was in Cyprus. The popular conception of Papandreou in the upper levels of the State Department was as a Svengali manipulating his aging and feeble father during the final years of the old man's otherwise distinguished political career. When American foreign service officers were assigned to Greece, one part of their indoctrination would often be a briefing on Andreas Papandreou. One U.S. diplomat being prepared for an important political assignment in Greece described his introduction to the subject:

> The Greek desk officer had handed me a large file folder of background material on Andreas prepared by the CIA which, among other things, purported to prove that he had been a fellow traveler if not worse for many years—since his student days—that he had engaged in corrupt practices during his membership in his father's government . . . that he was morally sinful . . . and that he was generally a most reprehensible individual who posed a serious danger to United States' interests in Greece.
>
> At the time I did not so much resent this effort to brainwash me about a person I had never met as I was somewhat astounded by the effort to discredit one individual in this fashion, an individual who, if guilty of all these crimes, would not be likely to beguile a fairly experienced officer like me for very long.

George Ball described the younger Papandreou as "that evil Andreas." Dean Acheson, who had attempted to mediate the Cyprus crisis of 1964, vented his annoyance with the Papandreous by describing them as "the old fool and the young rascal." Acheson's wrath was kindled by George Papandreou's refusal to accept his plan for resolving the crisis through a partition of the island, with the Greeks achieving union with the mother country and the Turks obtaining a military base on the northern edge of the island. Former U.S. Ambassador Ellis Briggs publicly denounced the Papandreous during the 1961 election campaign and praised Karamanlis, long the American favorite. Norbert Anschuetz, the Deputy Chief of Mission of the U.S. embassy in Athens advised Ambassador Talbot some weeks before the 1967 coup that if the Center Union party won the elections scheduled for May 1967, Andreas would probably abolish the monarchy, pull Greece out of NATO, and purge the Hellenic military forces to his political advantage.

How ironic it was that the first two of these steps were taken seven years later under Karamanlis, the conservative, after the overthrow of the junta in 1974.

The roots of American antipathy toward the younger Papandreou are complex—a mixture of personal pique and political motive. Prior to his return to Greece in 1959, Andreas was unknown to many in the American diplomatic community. Those who did know of him tended to regard him as a fellow American. He held U.S. citizenship. He spent the two most formative decades of his life in the United States. There he earned high standing as an academic economist who counted among his circle of friends many liberal Democratic intellectuals and politicians, such as John Kenneth Galbraith, Walter Heller, Carl Kaysen, and Hubert H. Humphrey. Some of them rose to high positions of influence in the Kennedy and Johnson administrations. Andreas Papandreou returned to Greece on leave from the University of California at Berkeley to establish a Center for Economic Research in Greece, funded by the Ford and Rockefeller Foundations. He was invited to start the center by Karamanlis. It would seem to have been an auspicious and totally respectable beginning for the political repatriation of Andreas Papandreou.

Of his many acquaintances in the American embassy at the time, Andreas wrote:

On the whole they were intelligent men. They took their work seriously; indeed they were literally immersed in it, so much so that in
most cases they had lost their detachment. They displayed the same
kind of emotional commitment to their pet political views that was
characteristic of the Greeks themselves. . . . Socially, the American
contingent belonged to the Greek establishment circle. They had
not necessarily sought this but they had been sought after. Yachts,
island vacations, sumptuous dinners, apartments in the countryside
were placed at their disposal by the Athenian elite. The Americans
could hardly refuse such courtesies but in this fashion they had
been literally assimilated by the ruling class. Their contacts with
the politicians who belonged to the Right were frequent and inti-
mate. In contrast, contacts with the Center deputies were infrequent
and strained.*

At the same time, even those Americans who agreed politically
with Andreas Papandreou acknowledged that he had become personally difficult during the years of growing mutual estrangement with
the American mission in Athens. Much was said of his arrogance, his
"paranoid" attitude toward the U.S. intelligence and military presence,
the stridency in his rhetoric, and the vitriol in his attitudes toward U.S.
policy and its agents in Greece. During an academic sabbatical from
his State Department duties, one former foreign service officer who
had once been a close friend of Andreas's wrote a paper—a psycho-
analytic critique—about Andreas. The paper argued that the younger
Papandreou was largely responsible for the 1967 military *coup d'état.*
Its theme was that Andreas's paranoid personality, his distant relationship with his father through childhood, his identity crisis of Greek
versus American nationality all caused him to behave in a way that
had polarized Greek politics and forced the colonels to intervene.

However, the crucial factor in the disintegration of relations between the Papandreous and the American establishment was not psychological but political. Both Papandreous were members of a species
of political leader with whom American foreign policy found itself at
odds during the 1960s and early 1970s. This species consisted of,
among others, Makarios in Cyprus, Sihanouk in Cambodia, Sukarno
in Indonesia, Brandt in West Germany, Allende in Chile, de Gaulle in
France, Bosch in the Dominican Republic, Goulart in Brazil. The
characteristic that these leaders held in common was that they chose

*Papandreou, *op. cit.,* p. 103.

to steer an independent course in their countries' internal development and foreign relations. In Greece, this meant collision with the well-entrenched military and intelligence arms of the American establishment as well as the diplomatic establishment.

Still, not everyone within the American embassy was hostile to young Papandreou. There were dissenting memoranda suggesting that his tirades against the influence of the CIA and the American military were motivated, in part, by his perceived need to purge himself of his American identity. From the time of his return, Andreas had been regarded as an imposter—a parachutist—in the Greek political scene. It was a theme used frequently by his enemies. Stories had also been circulated that he was in the pay of American intelligence services. In view of the general penetration of Greek political life by the Foreign Factor, no theory of double or even triple agentry could be deemed too preposterous for belief. And so, according to one friendly analyst within the embassy, Andreas was staking out a position for himself to the left of the established Center Union politicians, including his own father, where there was a large and untapped constituency for his reformist social doctrines and his denunciation of foreign incursions into Greek domestic affairs.

In American political terms, the younger Papandreou was a liberal Democrat whose views and speeches would have caused few ripples at the Universities of California or Minnesota, where he had taught, or even at Harvard, where he had studied, but that sounded like heresy in a Greece that was still dominated by the palace, the military, and the intelligence services.

There is one illustrative episode that got little attention in the United States but caused a journalistic furor in Athens. On March 1, 1967, in the final weeks of the caretaker government preceding the coup, two American diplomats went to hear a speech by Andreas at the regular weekly luncheon of the Foreign Press Association. Mimeographed copies of the speech were routinely handed out during the luncheon. The two U.S. officials, Political Officer John Day and Richard Helgerson of the United States Information Service, scanned the text and concluded on the basis of their quick perusal that it was so anti-American that they could not properly sit through its delivery. The two Americans walked out.

Years later, Day reaffirmed his belief in the correctness of his and Helgerson's action. "I just didn't think it was appropriate for an officer of the U.S. government to sit through the speech and listen to the allegations he made—not only about the American role in Greece, but such questions as how blacks were being treated in the United States, and so forth," Day recalled in an interview.

The walkout by Day and Helgerson caused a furor in the Athens press the next day. Quick to read official omens in the behavior of American officials, the Greek newspapers reported the incident with heavy headlines and speculated that the walkout had been intended to signal U.S. governmental disapproval of Andreas Papandreou. The right-wing press applauded the walkout. It further confirmed Andreas's suspicions of U.S. persecution.

The speech was a polemic against American foreign policy from Andreas's unusual perspective as a Greek leftist and American liberal. He said that the deeply pluralistic American society needed to achieve a balance of power among its contending interest groups for its foreign policies to function. He went on to say that the balance of forces was missing in foreign policy matters because of the apathy toward the whole subject felt by most Americans. As a result, the argument went, there were three forces which tended to dominate the American foreign policy process:

> First the Pentagon, which with the advent of the Cold War shaped American foreign policy as a policy of containment of the Soviet bloc. It gave emphasis to strategic considerations in all dealings of the United States with other nations. Second, the CIA which, as an outgrowth of the Office of Strategic Services which functioned during the Second World War as the key war intelligence unit—expanded beyond all expectations, assumed responsibilities and functions way beyond the initial purposes of the organization, and established an independence from the control of the government that made it possible for it practically to chart a parallel foreign policy for the United States. Last, but not least, the American investors abroad and the exporters to the world market played an important role as a pressure group in the formulation of American foreign policy.
>
> Under the circumstances it is not surprising that a military, bureaucratic, intelligence-oriented and business-dominated foreign policy failed to keep pace with the democratic developments at home.
>
> It does not come to us as a surprise to learn that America is going through an internal upheaval. The Negro problem is one cause, but there is probably a deeper cause, which underlies the conflict around the Negro problem and the foreign policy problem. It is that Amer-

ica is not living up to American ideals. And it is felt mostly by the intellectuals and by young people who come straight from the history books, who have been imbued with democratic principles. . . . For them, American presence in Vietnam is an error of the first degree, and American involvement in the internal affairs of other nations intolerable.

Had the speech been uttered in the United States in the course of a presidential campaign or at a National Press Club luncheon, it would have passed without remark. But Athens was not as politically tolerant as Washington. In the eyes of some official Americans, Papandreou was seen as a traitor and renegade for making such speeches. He was challenging, after all, some of the basic premises of American policy in Greece. It meant little to the American establishment in Athens that the positions taken by Andreas on the major issues of Greek domestic and foreign policy reflected the growing popular consensus in his country. Greek public opinion in the mid-sixties was running counter to the interests of the entrenched institutions of palace, army, intelligence service, and the counterpart American presence. Andreas was viewed by some of his former friends and acquaintances in the American embassy as a renegade—an American Lord Haw-Haw.

4. The Vise Tightens

The fourteen months of the 1964-1965 government of George Papandreou were a period of growing political turbulence, with the contradictions sharpening between the new Center Union government and the aggregate forces of the palace, the military, the politicians of the Right and, finally, the Americans. U.S. Ambassador Henry Labouisse, a Kennedy appointee, sought to open lines to the Papandreous and break away from the heavy patron-client relationship that had characterized the embassy's dealings earlier. For example, Labouisse alerted Papandreou after a group of senior Greek officers sought his views on U.S. attitudes toward a *coup d'état* after the departure of Karamanlis. The idea was to prevent George Papandreou from taking power in the 1964 election. Labouisse cabled Washington of his disapproval of the prospective coup and the State Department concurred.

The first major crisis of the new government was bred in Cyprus. The fragile constitutional arrangements negotiated under the gun at London and Zurich, designed to keep a tenuous balance between the Greek majority and Turkish minority in the new Cypriot state, had broken down. Cypriot President Archbishop Makarios, claiming that the repeated vetoes of the Turkish minority had brought about a condition of government paralysis, proposed thirteen amendments to the Constitution, including ending the veto power that the Turkish minority considered to be its political insurance policy.

The Turkish government summarily rejected the Makarios initiative on December 16, 1963, and withdrew from the government. Within five days violence erupted between the Turkish and Greek Cypriots. From the U.S. standpoint, the overriding concern was to prevent full-scale war from breaking out between the respective home countries, Greece and Turkey, the guardians of NATO's southern flank. Makarios was seen from Washington as a leader of dubious loyalties whose championship of nonalignment and overtures toward Moscow and other Communist capitals were viewed with suspicion. Cyprus was considered by some higher-level American policymakers as a potential Mediterranean Cuba and Makarios as a red priest. (Later, we will take a closer look at the American role in the Cyprus crisis.)

The immediate response of the United States was to try to extend the writ of NATO to Cyprus, while at the same time applying the severest diplomatic sanctions against Turkey to prevent it from invading the island. Papandreou riled senior American officials, among them Secretary of State Dean Rusk, Undersecretary of State George Ball, Special Mediator Dean Acheson, and others, because he stood stubbornly against American pressures to accept a partition plan for Cyprus. The elder Papandreou, who had been invited to Washington for the famous persuasion therapy of President Johnson, delivered a blunt lecture to Rusk aboard the presidential yacht. Referring to the proposal by Special Envoy Dean Acheson for the carving-up of Cyprus into a Greek majority holding and a Turkish base, Papandreou said, as reported by an observer, "It's okay for you to work up a brilliant plan. What you are saying is that I have to tell my people to shed Greek blood. You want me to whip Makarios and the Greek Cypriots into shape. I've got the army to shoot them with. You may be ready to do it, but I'm not. I am, it seems, a victim of the arrogance of power."

One senior State Department analyst summarized Washington's attitude toward the Greek prime minister in these terms: "Rusk and Company were disgusted with Papandreou. He was saying there was no such thing as a neat and simple solution."

Andreas, who accompanied his father on the trip to Washington, recalled President Johnson's demeanor at the White House:

> He acted as if he had not heard a word that anyone else had spoken. It was clear that he had been briefed, and that he was unwilling to depart one iota from his briefing. I could sense my father's desperation. His logic, his carefully prepared arguments were useless.

Johnson had a line: that he, Papandreou, should meet with [Turkish Premier] Inonu, that summit level negotiation should take place. Nothing Papandreou would say could change Johnson's mind. It had not been a discussion. It had been a monologue.*

President Johnson had been just as forceful with the Turks, however, and had sent Inonu a letter warning that in the event that Turkish forces invaded the island, the country might have to risk the consequences of Soviet reprisal unaided by the United States or other NATO "allies." In the end, the Turks backed away from a full-scale military confrontation but moved their population into enclaves to avoid harm from the Greek-Cypriot militia as well as to give support to the case for geographic division. But the Cyprus crisis of 1964 left a bitter taste in the mouths of the leaders of Greece, Turkey, Cyprus, and the United States. Conditions remained highly volatile.

From the right-wing press, a series of vitriolic attacks began against Andreas Papandreou for his role in the Cyprus dispute. Charges were circulated that he held primary responsibility for the Greek rejection of one version of the Acheson proposal that would have achieved political union with Greece for at least the major portion of the island. The fashionable epithet for Andreas among his detractors on the Right and in the Middle was "the parachutist of Greek politics." By May 1965, Andreas was implicated by General George Grivas, the hero of the Cyprus independence war, in an alleged military conspiracy by an order of officers who called themselves Aspida ("shield"). The Aspida affair was brought to light on Cyprus by Grivas, who transmitted authenticating documents to the top military command in Athens. The insurgent officers, according to evidence transmitted by Grivas, regarded Andreas as the future leader of Greece. The Aspida case brought to the surface the opposing forces in the Greek government. It became a vehicle for the right-wing military, in concert with King Constantine and Minister of Defense Petros Garoufalias, to harass the two Papandreous and was an important factor in their political downfall. Papandreou, ironically, was accused of using the KYP to purge the army of rightist elements. George Papandreou finally forced the issue by asking the King to sign a decree firing Garoufalias. The King refused. A constitutional crisis erupted, and there

*Papandreou, *op. cit.,* p. 134.

began between the King and Papandreou an exchange of letters that
resulted in Papandreou's decision to resign and force a new election.
"I do not accept the role of a humiliated prime minister, and I do not
consent to the violation of the principles of crown democracy," Papandreou wrote the King in his final letter. A new government was
sworn in by the King, drawn from Papandreou's own Center Union
colleagues. Papandreou denounced them as "traitors" and launched
the second "unrelenting struggle."

5. The Plan to Buy the Election

By early 1967, the stage was set again for new elections, which were widely expected to be a replay of the 1964 electoral outcome, only perhaps now with an even bigger majority for George Papandreou. Among the diplomats in the embassy, there were reports that the CIA had taken a preelection poll that indicated that the strength of the conservatives (the ERE, or National Radical Union, party) had fallen to a 20 or 25 percent level, while Papandreou's apparent margin of victory was now considerably higher than the 53 percent he had won three years earlier. King Constantine feared that a Center Union victory of such magnitude, reinforced by his own dismissal of the Papandreou government in 1965, could well portend the end of the monarchy.

One interesting and paradoxical political current as the election approached was the seepage of traditional Communist party supporters into the Center Union bandwagon of the Papandreous. It was a trend that did not escape the internal political reporting of the CIA. Communist party leaders were infuriated at the erosion of their ranks, and unlike 1964 when they instructed their adherents to support the Center Union in districts where they had no chance of their own, the party planned in 1967 to put up its candidates in every district.

The dominant American view, both in the diplomatic and CIA

wings of the embassy, was one of growing alarm at the prospect that a Papandreou victory—which seemed increasingly certain—would elevate Andreas Papandreou to a position of unparalleled influence in Greece's immediate political future. A senior intelligence official whose views weighed heavily in the formulation of the embassy's position on the so-called Papandreou threat summarized the situation this way:

> There was growing concern in our embassy that in an election Papandreou would win and Andreas would become the dominant figure. He had become increasingly anti-American. He was charging openly that Greece had lost her sovereignty to NATO which was an instrument of United States policy. Greece was agitated over the Cyprus situation and there were many who wanted to fight the Turks more than anyone else.
>
> Andreas was complaining that Greek national security requirements were being subordinated to NATO and American interests [and that] Greece was not able to meet its security requirements in Cyprus, for example, as a result of American manipulation of NATO. He said NATO and Greece had become instruments of United States policy, not Greek policy. He attacked the United States, KYP and CIA.
>
> The old man was now senile and if he were elected, Andreas would become more influential than ever. We were increasingly concerned about the election. We were concerned that if Papandreou won, Andreas would be in the driver's seat for all practical purposes. He would withdraw Greece from NATO, evacuate the United States bases, shut down the Communication Center at Nea Makri [a major U.S. naval communications facility near Marathon]. Andreas was also charging that the Americans corrupted the Greek economy. His answer would be to restrict the American presence and demand a high price for what remained.
>
> There was another concern: If the Papandreous won, there would be a Greek military coup. Andreas Papandreou made it clear that he considered the top military figures his enemies. No doubt the military was getting nervous.

At this stage, CIA Station Chief Maury and the top echelons of the diplomatic staff in the embassy converged on Talbot with a joint proposal for an extraordinary act of intervention by the United States. (Talbot, it must be noted, had been sticking to the Washington guidance, which was to oppose any "extraconstitutional" moves by the King designed to block the election.)

As Maury later described the incident:

Some members of the embassy staff suggested the possibility of a covert operation by the CIA to encourage and support the candidacy of moderate pro-Western elements who could strengthen the anti-Papandreou forces by winning over some of the fence-sitters.

The initial reaction of the American Ambassador, Phillips Talbot, to this proposal was ambivalent. For a deep believer in both the evils of military dictatorship and the sinfulness of CIA covert operations, it was not any easy choice.

However, as tensions mounted and rumors multiplied, senior members of the CIA country team met in January, 1967, for a detailed examination of the problem. We concluded that a victory by the Papandreous would seriously damage vital U.S. interests in the eastern Mediterranean area, weaken the southern flank of NATO and seriously destabilize the delicate Greek/Turkish relations then severely strained by the Cyprus situation. These conclusions were reported to the ambassador, who, after some prodding by members of his staff, agreed to recommend to Washington a modest covert program to support liberal or moderate pro-western candidates in a few electoral "swing" districts.

Reluctantly, Talbot sent a cable to Washington recommending that the CIA, as one official described the message, "be directed to undertake political action to head off a Papandreou victory." The proposal, specifically, was that $100,000 be authorized to the agency to subsidize some dozen candidates in swing districts, thereby drawing from Papandreou's prospective parliamentary strength.

In Washington, the request went to the National Security Council Committee on Covert Action—then the 303 Committee, now the 40 Committee—and was turned down. The Johnson administration was now at the peak of its involvement in Vietnam, for one thing. In addition, the newspapers of the United States were full of unraveling disclosures of CIA involvement in funding American student, labor, agricultural, and other organizations through prestigious foundation conduits, and the White House was smarting under the controversy. The fear of the national security managers back home was that the plan might backfire, and the risks outweighed the benefits.

The proposal for clandestine intervention to influence the outcome of the May 1967 election in Greece was, nonetheless, a confession of the bankruptcy of American diplomacy in Greece at that crucial moment. For Talbot, it must have been a trying episode, since the ambassador later spoke of himself as a force for lowering the high profile of the CIA in Greece, indeed, of the entire American presence. He was trying to continue in the pattern set by Labouisse, breaking away from the heavy patron-client relationship that had characterized the embassy's relations with the Greek ruling elite through the 1950s. That, at least, was how Talbot subsequently saw his role. But Talbot, like his boss, Dean Rusk, was a man of opaque manner; and if he was tormented by the decision of February 1967, his behavior showed nothing of it to his staff at the time.

As far as Washington was concerned, its rejection of the CIA covert political operation was not, by any evidence, dictated· by philosophical scruple. The same set of national security managers in the Johnson administration had heartily endorsed massive covert programs in the 1964 presidential election in Chile in support of Christian Democrat Eduardo Frei and in the overthrow of the Goulart leftist administration in Brazil by a military junta. In 1965, there was also the full-scale American political and military intervention in the Dominican Republic.

There was another course open to the American mission, a new initiative to mend relations with the Papandreous and their center-left constituency. Whatever might be thought of their policies, they were clearly riding the crest of popular opinion. It was an approach that was being recommended by a dissident minority on the American mission staff. But their memoranda were, by and large, being filed in the discard trays of the senior embassy officers, often with the ambiguous bureaucratic notation, "Noted." The adversary voices and policy drafts rarely got to Talbot's desk, let alone to the desks of the higher-level decisionmakers in the State Department or White House.

By late March and April, King Constantine was privately seeking the embassy's guidance on the U.S. attitude toward an "extraparliamentary" solution to the prospect of a Papandreou victory in the May 29 election. This meant nothing less than a coup by the military under the sanction of the King. Talbot struggled with the question and, finally, a staff memorandum was prepared reflecting the collective thinking of himself, Maury, Deputy Chief of Mission Norbert Anschuetz, Political Counselor Kay Bracken, and the embassy's internal Political Officer, John Day.

The draft was a classic piece of bureaucratic committee work. It reviewed the contingencies and reiterated Washington policy guidelines against at least public endorsement of "extraconstitutional" tactics. Finally, the document stated, in a masterstroke of ambiguity, that the American response to a coup effort by the King "would depend on the circumstances."

During the week of April 17, one member of the embassy staff began drafting a memorandum to Political Counsellor Bracken. Because of the prophetic clarity with which the memo foresaw the prospects of a coup coming before rather than after the election and the inattention that the memorandum received in the higher levels of the embassy from Bracken upward, it is worth reciting here. On the evening of April 20, the author of the draft completed and deposited it in an office safe to await typing. It said in part:

> I feel compelled to offer these thoughts on the present political crisis because I sincerely believe that the direction in which we are heading is extremely dangerous at a minimum and potentially disastrous for American interests in Greece. Specifically, it seems to me that the odds very heavily favor the imposition of a dictatorship as the resolution of the present crisis; and I fear that a dictatorship "solution" now will ultimately end in another Dominican Republic disaster for us. . . . Important political elements—the Palace, the ERE, hard core, the military, the conservative establishment—are determined that they will not permit the Papandreous to come to power.

The draft continued through a detailed analysis of the options open to the anti-Papandreou power coalition, suggesting that the two most likely tactics would be "open electoral fraud" that would have to be on a scale "obvious to everyone" or postponement of the election by force.

Instead of the ambiguous wording of the Talbot memorandum, which said that American response to a coup would "depend on the circumstances," this draft recommended a strong and unequivocal statement to the King: "We must make our position clear *now* on how we stand on the dictatorship question. If we are opposed, we must do our utmost to get that idea across now."

The draft concluded:

> The pro-dictatorship group would be unlikely to give us much or any advance warning that they were moving into a constitutional deviation. They could guess that we might be opposed to the idea, and they would therefore wish to present us with a *fait accompli*, assuming that we would eventually have to accept a *de facto* situation. We might wake up one morning, say three weeks from now, to find a dictatorship already installed and functioning. . . .

The prediction came true not in three weeks but in twelve hours. The draft was still in its author's office on the morning of April 21, when the tanks swept into Athens proclaiming the "revolution" of the colonels, when Andreas Papandreou had already been hauled off to jail and his father placed under house arrest, and when CIA Station Chief Maury was being detained at a military roadblock.

6. The Wrong Coup

"We were looking at the wrong coup," said a State Department official who had served in Athens for many years, and was there the morning of April 21, 1967. "We were caught off guard."

The American embassy was a picture of confusion as Talbot and his staff tried to sort out the origins and leaders of the smoothly executed insurrection that was under way in the streets outside.

Maury's staff in the CIA station had learned that detailed advance planning had been undertaken under the direction of Greece's highest-ranking military officer, General Gregory Spandidakis, for a military takeover of the government. All the paperwork had been completed —code name, unit maneuvers, public declarations, staging grounds, all the logistical groundwork for the coup. The takeover was to be ordered by King Constantine on the grounds that he had to preserve the monarchy and the nation in the face of the imminent threat from its enemies—presumably, Papandreou and the Communists. The military code name was *Ierax* ("Hawk").

"Our intelligence reporting," said one official source, "as one would expect in reports prepared by the technicians of coups—dealt far more with the details of the plans for carrying it out than with the political content once they were in power. . . . In other words, we knew a great deal about who would take over and how, but little about what they would do with the power once it was theirs." But it was irrelevant. "Hawk" never flew.

It was apparent on the day of the coup that the king had nothing to do with the surprise takeover. Neither the Joint U.S. Military Assistance Group (JUSMAGG) nor the military attaché's office were of much use in providing background on the coup group and its leaders, George Papadopoulos, Stylianos Pattakos, and Nicholas Makarezos. The diplomatic staff, goaded by frantic cables from Washington for facts and assessments, turned to the CIA staff. Harris Greene, Maury's deputy, dug out a report from the previous January that identified a group of officers headed by a Colonel George Papadopoulos who were associated with a military fraternal group known by the acronym EENA, a splinter of the main Greek military order, IDEA (the Sacred Bond of Greek Officers). The report said that the Papadopoulos group was plotting to overthrow the civilian government.

But there was something peculiar about the CIA reporting on the Papadopoulos group. It stopped in January. Another curious fact was that Papadopoulos had been Director of Counterintelligence for the KYP at the time Maury arrived in Greece in 1962 and was, presumably, well known at least to middle-level CIA officials, who maintained close liaison with their KYP counterparts to the extent of sharing the same building space in Athens.

In Washington, a veteran analyst of the State Department's Office of Intelligence and Research (INR), a Greek American named Charilaos Lagoudakis, was also intrigued by the January report and perplexed by the sudden halt of CIA information on what seemed to be a serious, middle-level military conspiracy.

On February 6, 1967, he submitted a memo to his superior, Philip Stoddard, head of the Near East Division of INR, a copy of which was obtained through nongovernmental sources. Perhaps it is too easy to say with hindsight that if the bureaucracy had responded to the warning inquiry of Lagoudakis, the Papadopoulos coup would have been avoided—or at least the embassy would not have been caught unawares on April 21. But the senior and respected analyst, who knew the politics of Greece as well as anyone in Washington and had occupied his job for some two decades, was telling the State Department, in effect, that the butler had announced his intention to commit the crime and was on his way to the master bedroom, loaded revolver in hand. Here is the memorandum in full:

THE RIGHT WING CONSPIRATORIAL GROUP
IN THE GREEK ARMED FORCES

Since June 19, 1965, RNA [Near East desk] has seen some 15 CIA
reports from various sources on the so-called "Rightist Greek Military Conspiratorial Group." The latest report was dated January 23,
1967. These reports state that the "conspiratorial group" is ready
to stage a military coup when, in its view, a dictatorship would become necessary as the only alternative to Center Union control of
Parliament.

Some twenty names of active and retired officers are mentioned
as key members of this military movement, prominent among whom
are Lt. Col. D. [*sic*] Papadopoulos and Lt. Col. D. Stamatelopoulos
[an original planner of the conspiracy who fell out with Papadopou-
los]. The "conspiratorial group" reportedly has existed since late
1963, but was presumably dispersed by Papandreou upon his acces-
sion to power in February, 1964. Papadopoulos reportedly said in
December, 1966, that "Once a dictatorship is established, it will seek
U.S. support in order to implement social and economic measures
which can deter the present tendency toward the left." The first
meeting of the "group" since the fall of the Stephanopoulos government [the government sworn in by the King after he dismissed
George Papandreou] allegedly was held on January 4, 1967. Col.
Papadopoulos was the principal speaker.

We have no information on this "conspiratorial group" from non-
CIA sources, and the available CAS [an official acronym for CIA:
Controlled American Source] information is very sketchy. Inasmuch
as army and Palace circles are reportedly concerned about the possibility of a Papandreou victory in the May elections, *it would be
useful to have further information on this rightist group which may
now be preparing for a possible coup. Perhaps discreet inquiries by
CAS and the Political Section might be in order.* (Emphasis added.)

Copies of the memo went to the State Department Greek Country
Director Dan Brewster and the department's CIA liaison office.
Lagoudakis also directed follow-up requests to the CIA for more
information. Presumably, these requests were channeled for action
to the CIA station in Athens. In any event, Papadopoulos and his co-
conspirators were in power in Athens before an answer could be
returned.

What accounted for this curious lapse in CIA reporting on the
colonels' group—particularly at a time when the agency was monitoring closely the palace plot that was being advanced by General

Spandidakis? Was it the distraction of too many coup schemes being hatched at one time? Or bureaucratic inertia? Or was it a cover-up by elements within the Athens station who wanted the Papadopoulos plot to succeed?

The one persistent line of speculation within the American diplomatic community in Athens is that there might have been a signal transmitted to the Papadopoulos group by a middle-level intelligence officer in a way to provide, in the later lexicon of Watergate, "plausible deniability." There was, at the middle level of the CIA station, a group of Greek-American operatives, many of whom had served in Greece since the days of the civil war. In that period, the CIA was helping to coordinate the battle by the royalist forces against the Communist-dominated EAM (National Liberation Front) movement, then comprising Greece's staunchest anti-Nazi cadres. One of the earliest American station chiefs was Thomas Karamessines, who rose through the ranks of the CIA to become Deputy Director for Plans, the head of clandestine operations. The Greek-American operatives in Athens had seen station chiefs come and go, as they had seen American policy fluctuate according to the vagaries of ambassadorial style and Washington attitudes. All the while, it was they who were mounting operations, nurturing and expanding their strings of agents, and cementing the relationship between the CIA and its counterpart, KYP, as well as the military and conservative party elements with whom they were ideologically allied.

"We were well aware of the problem of the so-called Greek Mafia," a former CIA executive acknowledged. "It was discussed at the CIA very often. We think we had it under control."

Yet, elsewhere in the embassy, U.S. diplomatic personnel looked askance at the anomaly of a large Greek-American staff serving as a sort of permanent operations group in the country of their origin. "In the foreign service, we often are not even assigned to a post if it happens to be the homeland of our wife's family," remarked a diplomatic officer with years of service in Greece. "But these guys are kept here not just for years but for decades. Needless to say, they've gotten very ingrown in the political milieu."

By and large, the group was ideologically right-wing, as much so as any of their military or intelligence counterparts in the Greek services. They were fiercely anti-Papandreou, regarding him as the preeminent apostle of the Greek Left. Furthermore, the Greek Americans were intimately connected with the leading figures in the KYP.

The leaders of the April 21, 1967, coup were the top men in the KYP: Papadopoulos himself, who had been Head of Counterintelligence; Nicholas Makarezos, Chief of Information; Michael Roufogalis, Director of Personnel. Dimitrios Ioannides, who eventually overthrew the Papadopoulos regime, was Chief of the Military Police.

The King's coup was reported to have been set for mid-May, within two weeks of the scheduled election. However, one of the palace conspirators, General George Zoitakis, was also in touch with the plotters of the colonels' coup. In his impatience to get the coup engine started, Zoitakis went to the Papadopoulos group and informed them of the timing and substance of the plans for the generals' coup—American intelligence sources learned long afterward. The colonels acted immediately.

It would seem that in view of the years of investment in penetrating and developing the KYP apparatus, it would not have been a remarkable feat of intelligence for the CIA station to have apprehended the Papadopoulos coup. For months, members of the Papadopoulos-EENA conspiracy had been moving into strategic positions around Athens. They organized new tactical units, took over such installations as the army tank school and key communications installations. The apparent inability of the CIA in Athens to maintain contact with some of its closest and most long-standing clients on the eve of their seizure of state power, in fact, probably stands as one of the most egregious intelligence failures in the CIA's history.

The questions that automatically arise are these: Did Papadopoulos succeed in breaking contact with the CIA monitoring process that produced the fifteen reports that had come to the attention of Lagoudakis in Washington? Or did the working-level operatives in Athens stop reporting on the activities of the colonels' group? Was the agency— or at least its second-level employees—trying to maintain the security of their counterpart network in Greece? Or, worse yet, did employees of the CIA station in Athens deliberately break contact with the Papadopoulos group in order not to give away in advance plans for a coup with which they were in total political sympathy?

Lagoudakis made the significant point in his memorandum that the only source of U.S. government reporting on the Papadopoulos coup group came from the CIA. There was one exception. Early in April, a right-wing member of Parliament, Nick Farmakis, mentioned to

U.S. Deputy Chief of Mission Anschuetz that a military coup was on its way—not the generals' coup, which the embassy was aware of, but a coup by a group of colonels who were personal friends of his. Farmakis, the only member of Parliament who openly described himself as a fascist, proclaimed himself to be in sympathy with the coup. No one of rank in the embassy's political section took Anschuetz's report of this meeting seriously. Afterward, Farmakis was one of the few pipelines of information for the embassy into the coup group. Anschuetz joked about ordering a crow from the Athens Hilton restaurant for the two skeptical political officers, Kay Bracken and John Day, to share. Had he been aware of the fifteen CIA reports that reached the desk of Lagoudakis in Washington, he might have been able to put the intelligence from the friendly fascist parliamentarian into a more serious perspective.

7. Policy on Ice

After the tanks of the junta rolled and the characters in the drama had been sorted out, Washington and Athens were in equal states of confusion over what to do next. In the embassy, there were those, including Maury, who wanted to make strong representations to Papadopoulos to withdraw from office and defer to the authority of King Constantine. The King contacted Talbot and the British embassy but got no hint of what strategies of resistance those governments would support. (Talbot did instruct American embassy personnel not to discuss the situation with their Greek friends, a suggestion that was greeted with derision by members of the staff but that was nonetheless one of the few positive acts to come out of the ambassador's office at the time.) Constantine was loath to deal directly with the coup makers, lowly colonels and unknowns as they were. He also was deeply angered by the beating given his devoted military aide Major Michael Arnaoutis by troops who arrested him.

Political Officer John Day was dispatched to Washington to find out what the views were in the higher levels of the State Department. He returned as much in the dark as when he had left, according to embassy colleagues. Another member of the mission who made a brief visit to Washington said of the mood in the capital, "At the White House and NSC [National Security Council] staff the feeling was: Let the Greeks have their military dictatorship. We have our hands full in Southeast Asia. We've been taking care of the Greeks too goddamned long. Let them stand on their own feet!"

In Athens, Maury and several members of the political section were separately, and for different reasons, telling Talbot that Papadopoulos was extremely vulnerable to American pressure and could be persuaded to withdraw in favor either of the King or of a caretaker government that would hold elections. Maury's professed position was a reflection of his close relationship with the royal family and a feeling of repugnance for the brutal and grubby colonels who were depicting themselves as saviors of their country.

He felt the answer was to go straight to Papadopoulos and tell him bluntly, "You men probably thought you were acting in the interests of your country. But make no mistake about it, the United States Government will not tolerate a continuation of the dictatorship. If you don't step aside and appoint a caretaker government by the fall, you've had it. We're going to get you."

Some ten days after the coup, the CIA Chief had, in fact, received a call from Papadopoulos, suggesting that they sit down for a drink. Because of their shared vocation of intelligence, the two men had been acquainted with each other in the precoup days. Maury informed Talbot of the contact and offered to see the otherwise incommunicative junta leader. Talbot, according to a reliable embassy source, said no. "I don't think the United States should conduct its affairs in dark alleys," the ambassador is reported to have told the Station Chief. Maury complied, but he later confided to a colleague in the embassy, "If I had that drink with Papadopoulos, I'm sure I could have scared the shit out of him."

With few exceptions, the U.S. military establishment in Athens warmed up quickly to the coup group. So did the major elements of the CIA's working-level staff, with Maury probably the least sympathetic member of the station to the new rulers. The upper level of the diplomatic side reflected Talbot's cautious ambivalence, cued by the prevailing tone of apathy and indecision at the Washington end of the cable traffic.

There were two major options for American policy at this juncture. One was active intervention to pressure the colonels to withdraw in favor of a caretaker government. This could have been pursued by such means as bringing the Sixth Fleet into visible range of the port city of Piraeus, cutting off military aid, recalling the ambassador, issuing public statements in Washington denouncing the colonels' resort to "extraconstitutional" action, and other such measures. The second course would have been to maintain a posture of neutrality, not recognizing the new ruling junta but not taking any public action that might be construed as a rebuke, while carrying on day-to-day relations and hoping to influence a return to some form of constitutional rule. The third option was full-scale recognition of the regime.

It was the second course, keeping all contingencies open and doing substantially nothing, that Talbot and his senior staff finally decided upon. In a cable to Washington, Talbot proposed that the embassy work out a *modus vivendi* for day-to-day relations in order to preserve both American and NATO interests in Greece. But as offsetting conditions, he suggested that the United States leave the question of diplomatic recognition moot and that the embassy stress the need to impress American opinion with the junta's intention to return to constitutional government as soon as possible. Talbot also recommended that "we utilize the dialogue regarding long-term MAP [Military Assistance Program] planning as a means of pressuring the government by installments to formulate and announce their program of evolution toward a constitutional regime."

The overall pattern of American response to Papadopoulos's coup sustained him in those early days. In the words of one senior U.S. official who was centrally involved in the events, "The ambivalence of Washington plus the professed desire of the military to continue business as usual left Papadopoulos with the impression that Washington was being quiet for politically cosmetic reasons and the Americans who counted—DOD [Department of Defense] and CIA— thought he was a great guy. He hung in and eventually got his way. The Greek population as a whole assumed that if the United States disapproved, it would have knocked Papadopoulos out." The Greeks were, after all, still under the spell of the Foreign Factor.

There were by now only two middle-level political officers in the embassy who favored action against Papadopoulos. Maury's position was determined primarily by his bias toward the palace. The new Greek rulers were upstarts and low-grade conspirators who, in the words of one analyst, advanced their careers not on the battlefield but "through political intrigue, through plotting, by working in intelligence and personnel, back-room types."

In the aftermath of the coup, Talbot did move quickly to achieve a partial suspension of American military aid, primarily of heavy equipment, to the new regime. He made his decision with the head of the military mission, General Eaton, as a cargo ship carrying a consignment of tanks bore down on the port city of Pireaus on the day of the coup.

The ambassador was appropriately concerned about the political consequences of a new batch of American tanks arriving on the docks of Piraeus to supplement the ones that had just extinguished the constitutional government of Greece. He recommended to Washington that the oncoming ship be diverted to Turkey and that another vessel bringing tanks and heavy weapons be unloaded in Italy until the situation in Athens became clearer. The suspension remained technically in effect until the National Security Council of the Nixon administration, under the chairmanship of Henry Kissinger, decided in the fall of 1969 to restore full-scale military assistance to the junta.

The irony of the on-the-spot decision by Talbot and Eaton to cut off the heavy arms shipments to the junta and the long, ensuing bureaucratic struggle in Washington to restore them deeply impressed the close-hand official observer of the episode who later reflected:

> Most of the executive branch in Washington, and especially the military, came to regret this suspension policy, for it later proved as difficult to reverse as it had been easy to impose in the heat of the coup crisis. It required years of exchanges of telegrams, memoranda, staff studies, presidential examinations, argument and counter argument, finally an NSC decision to reverse a "policy" that was reached with very little consideration by Eaton and Talbot in a conference lasting only a few minutes, since the proper course of action at the time was obvious to everyone: We don't want those tanks paraded through the streets of Athens "right now."

To the high-ranking American military officers in Athens, the new military rulers in Greece were upstanding, anti-Communist, pro-NATO, pro-American counterparts. General David Burchinall, Commander of the United States armed forces in Europe, fired off cable after cable to Washington, urging restoration of aid to the new regime. "The greatest government since Pericles," proclaimed one senior U.S. Commander in Europe. General Andrew Goodpaster, then Commander of NATO forces, arrived in Athens and posed smiling beside Papadopoulos for newspaper photographs.

Through the summer of 1967, the American embassy in Athens floundered along with a policy of ambivalence while Papadopoulos shrewdly purged the military of potential opposition. Constantine was unable to get a clear indication of what help he might expect from the Americans, who in the past had been only too willing to foist their views on the palace. He reluctantly swore in the Papadopoulos government and bided his time. At this point a new military confrontation was building up between the Israelis and the Arab states. On the scale of American priorities Greece reverted to its traditional role as a military base for Middle East and southern European crises. Administration witnesses before congressional committees kept stressing the importance of Greece as a logistical asset for the defense of Israel in future Middle East conflict. The dubiousness of such arguments was immediately questioned by congressional critics familiar with the political geography of the East Mediterranean. Greece clearly could not tilt publicly toward Israel because of its substantial interests in the Arab states. The argument was aimed, nonetheless, at the liberal Democratic, pro-Israeli forces on Capitol Hill. One target in particular was Congressman Benjamin Rosenthal (D-New York), whose House Foreign Affairs European Subcommittee was a standing forum of opposition in Congress to the rule of the junta in Athens.

In any event, Greece fell off the front pages while the six-day war preoccupied the administration and the foreign policy bureaucracy.

And so the U.S. foreign policy process insofar as it concerned Greece was put on ice while the next important episode took shape in Athens, one that served more than any other event since the coup to consolidate the power of the colonels. It was the pathetic, almost ludicrous, attempt by young King Constantine to stage a countercoup against Papadopoulos—a failure that was sealed by the indifference, or neutrality or duplicity, of the American embassy—depending on the viewpoint of the beholder.

8. Countercoup

Constantine, an avid sailor, traveled to the United States in late August 1967 to watch the America's Cup regatta at Newport but, more important, to get a firsthand exposure to Washington's attitude toward the developments in his country. Though he enjoyed the races, there was little consolation to be found in the muggy American capital and particularly in Foggy Bottom, the site of State Department headquarters, and on Capitol Hill. The King was trying to determine the extent of support in Washington for a stand against the Papadopoulos regime. Instead of support, however, he found himself being taxed personally for the regime in power in Athens. At one point, he exclaimed helplessly, "It's not *my* government." Nonetheless, some congressional liberals who followed Greek affairs could not forget that it was he who had precipitated the July 1965 constitutional crisis by dismissing Papandreou's government and, in effect, starting the chain of events that led to the coup. This was to be the chief criticism of the King's role in the events that in the eyes of many junta critics led inexorably to the 1967 colonels' coup.

Nonetheless, the King continued to try to reach out into the Greek political community and into the military for support in an effort against the junta. The leading Center Union party leader, George Mavros, was promoting a plan, which was kept in strict secrecy, among those who were sympathetic to the idea of the King's reclaiming power. Under the scheme, the King, after sending his family abroad, would go north to Salonika on December 13 and rally the military commanders in the north to his side. The bulk of Greece's military strength was in the northern district where it could be deployed quickly to the Turkish border or against invasion by a Balkan neighbor in conformity with Greece's NATO role. Then the King would announce to the country that he was accepting the resignation of the Papadopoulos government, of which the technical head was then Prime Minister Kollias. The colonels would have no recourse but to bow to the superior military strength at the King's disposal. He would thank them for their services but tell them they were no longer necessary, since a new constitution had been submitted. An amnesty would be declared for both the coup leaders and their victims, by then many thousands of political prisoners. An interim government of senior military leaders loyal to the King would be installed, continuing the existing state of martial law. Then, in due time, the King would replace the military government with a new one comprised of the outstanding political figures from all segments of the country's political life—men such as Karamanlis on the conservative side, George Papandreou from the Center Left, and Kanellopoulos from the Center Right. They, in turn, would serve as a transitional government and prepare the way for new national elections, which would be conducted as a model of fairness. It was expected that the United States would support the King's effort to reclaim power.

But the planning, such as it was, for the King's countercoup was interrupted by a new crisis in Cyprus. The November 1967 Cyprus crisis began when General George Grivas, then sixty-six and still a national hero because of his leadership of the guerrilla war in Cyprus in the fifties, staged new attacks against two Turkish-Cypriot villages, killing more than two dozen Turks. The action enraged the Turks, as had the earlier excesses in 1964. Within a week, there was every indication that the Turks were prepared to invade Cyprus, raising again the specter of all-out war between the two guardians of NATO's southern flank.

President Johnson dispatched his former Secretary of the Army, Cyrus Vance, who worked round-the-clock for ten days, shuttling between the three crisis capitals. Vance, as intermediary, helped to negotiate a solution that actually involved a major and humiliating capitulation by the Greek junta—the removal of the 6,000 Greek forces illegally smuggled into Cyprus since 1964 in violation of the

London-Zurich agreements. These were the international accords under which the sovereign Cypriot state was established in 1960. The Greeks had forced a test of strength on the island for which they had no commensurate military power. It was a sad day in the Greek Pentagon when the troops returned after the Cyprus settlement and Grivas was recalled to Greece for a nominal form of house arrest. It could not be disguised as anything but a surrender to Ankara.

Emboldened by the turn of events, the King's planning was intensified. He continued to test the will of the Americans through contacts with Talbot and also Maury. By early December, the junta forced the King's hand. Papadopoulos, who had been carefully pruning the military ranks of royalist supporters, now planned to retire en masse a large group of officers who were considered loyal to the crown. This would be precisely the sort of constituency in the armed forces that the King would need to carry out his plan.

Maury was concerned that Constantine was failing to plan realistically for the countercoup. He pleaded with Talbot to cross-examine the King on whether he had staffed out his plans. What was his communications plan? What radio station would he use to get his message across? What airfields had he planned to use if he got into trouble? What was he doing about security in keeping the operation secret from the ever present agents of KYP and Papadopoulos? As it turned out, these were all the right questions—particularly the last one.

Talbot responded that obtaining this information was not his role as the American ambassador. "It would be interfering," he countered. "We would become a party to it."

"We are a party to it already," Maury answered. "You would be increasing your responsibility just by saying, 'Go with God.' "

The King did not tell the American ambassador of his final plans until the eve of the coup, when he mentioned in lowered voice at a party in Athens that he had something of extreme importance to communicate. Would Talbot come to his country palace at Tatoi the following morning? The ambassador agreed. As recounted by one American official well acquainted with the records and with King Constantine's movements during that period, the King told Talbot at Tatoi that he had decided to move against Papadopoulos. The wheels would be set in motion within minutes, before Talbot even had a chance to get back to Athens.

"I have a request to make of you," Constantine went on. "Here is a tape of my message to the people. Please arrange to have it broadcast on the Voice of America." All he was asking of the Americans, he said, was to have the Sixth Fleet make an appearance in Phaleron Bay where it would be publicly visible. "Finally if my family is in mortal danger, I hope you assist in their evacuation. . . . I am not asking for the same sort of thing that was done in Lebanon, the landing of Marines. I simply ask for your help in getting the message out."

The ambassador took the King's tape-recorded message, but it was never broadcast on the Voice of America. According to some intelligence sources, the only broadcasting the King may have done that day was into the hidden tape recorders of KYP agents during his meeting with Talbot. The junta had the King under its eye day by day, hour by hour. The royal family was under surveillance when they left for Salonika, staging ground for the coup, with the pets, the nursemaids, the Queen's obstetrician, the Queen Mother, dozens of trunks, two airplanes, and Prime Minister Kollias, who was defecting to the King's side.

Up to the point of the countercoup, according to one diplomatic source, the Americans had been telling the King, "Your Majesty, you are the only person who can pull this together. You have the full good wishes and support of the United States." But the King, unfortunately, interpreted the word *support* in a different way from what was intended.

The operational phase of the King's pitiable coup effort took just a few hours to fail, all at the sufferance of the junta. The royalist side controlled the regular Salonika radio for a couple of hours, during which the message was broadcast to the generals in the north who were to support the effort. Then the junta took possession of the radio. Constantine, in a gesture of ill-timed *noblesse oblige*, sent one of his generals to the Greek Pentagon with a letter to General Angelis, chief of the armed forces under the junta, relieving him of his command and appointing the bearer of the message to succeed him. Angelis put the hapless royalist general in jail as soon as he read the letter from the King. In the north, the King's generals did arrest some of the junta's spies and operatives under their command. But once the junta officers pledged their loyalty to the King, they were released and pressed into service. The Papadopoulos agents, acting according to plan, then arrested the senior officers who had proven in the most blatant way their disloyalty to the junta. In this manner, Papadopou-

los was able, through the instrument of the countercoup, to identify
and jail the remaining royalist supporters in the upper echelons of the
Hellenic armed services. They, not by coincidence, were also the most
dedicated pro-NATO members of the Greek officer corps and had the
closest contacts with the Americans. The corps was now thoroughly
decimated.

In ignominy, the King and his enormous personal retinue fled to
Italy. He had chosen December 13 to make his move under the impression that it was his lucky day. But in Greek superstition, as in our
own, thirteen is regarded as a number of decidedly bad luck. Efforts
by the embassy in Athens to find out what was going on were complicated by the fact that the American Consul-General was off hunting
in Yugoslavia and his deputy had just driven to Athens to buy liquor
from the commissary for his own and his colleagues' larders. In the
evacuated palace, the junta found the discarded letters of support for
the King from the civilian leaders such as Karamanlis and Papandreou,
who had pledged to play their part in the royal insurgency under the
general terms of the plan endorsed by Mavros. Afterward, the King
would tell an American confidant:

> The impression I had was that not only would your country be in
> my corner but that you would have planes and ships off-shore—that
> you would make it clear the United States was hoping for a return
> to democracy and would broadcast the tape I gave to the Ambassa-
> dor. Beyond that, I assumed there were other ways you could exert
> influence without being identified.
>
> From your ambassador I got the impression that the United States
> would not remain indifferent, that there would be a showing of
> American interest.

The day was to provide a painful postscript for Talbot as well. After
the American Ambassador returned to Athens, with the wobbly
wheels of the countercoup already in motion, he received word that
Papadopoulos wanted to see him. There was an insistent tone in the
newly self-installed Prime Minister's message. Talbot, with a strong
sense of foreboding, went to the meeting in the company of his internal Political-Reporting Officer, John Day, who was to take notes and
serve as a witness. Papadopoulos went immediately to the subject of
the coup: What did Talbot know about the King's schemes? More
important, what had he been doing at Tatoi that morning conferring

with Constantine? Whose side was the American ambassador on, anyway? The ambassador nervously bobbed and parried. He was now in the thankless position of having incurred the long-term disfavor of both sides: the King and his civilian cohorts for not having provided the modicum of visible support for which they were hoping and the regime of the colonels for having appeared to be colluding with Constantine. Even had the ambassador wished to cooperate with the King's scheme, he was now exposed, and it was becoming increasingly evident that the junta had his every move recorded, perhaps literally.

One U.S. diplomatic observer and participant concluded afterward, "Whether or not he realized it at the moment, his [Talbot's] usefulness as the American ambassador to Greece was all but wiped out that very day; the junta never trusted him again, considered him implicated in the effort to oust them from power, and had no use at all for him from that day forward." Yet, Talbot was kept in the post for an additional year, a diplomatic paraplegic reduced almost to the pure formalities of ambassadorial representation.

9. The Arms Cutoff

The American heavy arms embargo, which started as a spur of the moment public relations gesture on the day of the coup, became the most visible instrument of political and diplomatic leverage applied by the United States during the transition from the Johnson to the Nixon administrations.

While the ostensible purpose of the embargo policy was to prod the junta into moving smartly toward restoration of constitutional government, the United States was continuing to supply the military regime with weapons—small arms, ammunition, and communications equipment—that were highly suitable for internal security and political repression. After the Soviet invasion of Czechoslovakia in the fall of 1968, the United States resumed for a time the delivery of heavy weapons, which had been curtailed in April 1967. Ostensibly, the reason was to enable Greece to protect itself against a Soviet or Soviet-inspired invasion. But as one respected American analyst of Greek affairs and former government official pointed out:

> Nobody suggested that Greece was in danger of a Soviet invasion; Russian troops might be sent to the lost sheep of the house of Lenin, but they would not cross the lines set at Yalta—any more than American troops would cross them in the other direction to defend the independence of a Hungary or a Czechoslovakia. Czechoslovakia would thus seem to be the excuse, rather than the reason, for the renewed shipment of heavy arms to Greece.*

*Richard Clogg and George Yannopoulos, *Greece Under Military Rule*. New York: Basic Books, 1972, p. 245.

In 1971, two staff investigators for the Senate Foreign Relations Committee, Richard Moose and James Lowenstein, concluded, after reviewing the military aid arithmetic of the embargo, that Greece had received larger amounts of overall military assistance during the three years and five months when the heavy arms embargo was in effect than in the equivalent period before it was imposed. They cited State Department figures that showed that in the three fiscal years during which the embargo was in effect, deliveries of military aid averaged $106.9 million a year. In the three fiscal years preceding the embargo, deliveries ran at about $95.2 million a year. This was explained by the fact that while American grant aid declined sharply during the supposed cutoff of military aid, there was a sharp rise in delivery of excess defense items and equipment provided under the foreign military sales program. The effect of the embargo was to provide Greece with weapons of the sort most suitable for internal repression while theoretically denying access to the sophisticated fighter planes and tanks suitable for a foreign war.

Nonetheless, the military leaders of the junta grumbled angrily at their American counterparts in Athens, and some members of the JUSMAGG mission were heard to complain during this period that the Greeks were boycotting their receptions. In Washington, the Defense Department and its allies in the State Department maintained a steady drumbeat of internal pressure for an end to the embargo in order to permit Greece to discharge its NATO obligations, whatever these might have been.

In July 1969, Secretary of State William Rogers assured the Senate Foreign Relations Committee that the suspension on heavy military aid would not be removed "unless the Greek junta made some progress toward more parliamentary government." Then Defense Secretary Melvin Laird told the committee during the same set of hearings:

> I want it understood at the present time we have a freeze on the aid as far as Greece is concerned, and that freeze is being continued and will be continued until progress is made toward more democratic procedures in that country. We have not released any military equipment to Greece since I have been Secretary of Defense, and the freeze is currently on the program as far as Greece is concerned. . . . Since this administration has been in office, there has been no relaxing, no relaxation of that freeze. We are hopeful that the Greek government will move in the direction of democratic procedures, and this would be reviewed at that time.

Another declaration of administration policy on the arms question was provided the following month by Assistant Secretary of State William B. Macomber, Jr., who said, in response to written expressions of congressional concern on the current Greek policy, that the administration was in a serious dilemma:

> On the one hand we see an autocratic government denying basic civil liberties to the citizens of Greece. . . . On the other hand, Greece is a NATO ally which has scrupulously fulfilled its treaty obligations [and] is important to our strategic interests in the Mediterranean area. . . . This, then, is the dilemma—how to deal with an ally with whose internal order we disagree yet who is a loyal NATO partner working closely with the United States in furtherance of the purposes and obligations of the NATO Treaty.
>
> Our policy toward Greece is now under intensive review. As we consider this difficult problem we will keep the suggestions of yourself and your colleagues very much in mind.

While the internal debate was in progress over the issue of resumption of arms shipments, reports began filtering out of Greece about torture as well as the arrest of thousands of political prisoners who had been rounded up in the aftermath of the coup. The investigation conducted by the Council of Europe unearthed the testimony of the victims of the new regime in Athens and circulated it around the world.

Petros Vlassis, a twenty-six-year-old student, gave this testimony, which was typical of the accounts of victims of the regime:

> . . . They poured water over me for a second time and they hit me. When I regained my senses, they bound me to the bench, but this time it was a different kind of torture, an individual one inflicted by Kravatiris. He hit me on the bones, starting with the ankles, then the legs and the knees. After that, he hit me on the genitals and he attempted to introduce the stick into my rectum.*

This is an excerpt from the account of Catherine Arseni, a thirty-four-year-old actress:

> First they lit matches in my eyes, [then] they stepped on my stomach. Spanos held my arm he pulled my hair and bumped my head

*Yearbook of the European Convention on Human Rights: The Greek Case, 1969. The Hague: Martinus Nijhoff, 1972, p. 208.

on the bench. All this time they were screaming and shouting . . .
dancing around me, interrogating me, insulting me and threatening
me. They told me they were going to throw me from The Terrace to
the street. That was the only thing that by that time I wished to
happen—to be dead. I was so ashamed. I was so frightened. Even
though the pain was unbearable sometimes, the fear and the shame
was the most dreadful thing I remember now.†

Such were the accounts of beatings, electric shock, *falanga* (beatings
administered to the soles of the feet), psychological torment, and in-
numerable other forms of torture that emerged during the European
Commission of Human Rights investigation of the Greek regime. The
inquiries were conducted under Article 3 of the European Convention
on Human Rights, which stated that "no one shall be subjected to
torture or to inhuman or degrading treatment or punishment." The
Council of Europe's investigating bodies heard testimony that prisoners of the regime had been crippled, driven insane, and killed during their incarceration in the various prisons of the junta government.
One of the facilities in which torture was being applied was the military police quarters within a block of the American embassy and not
far from the statue that had been erected to President Harry Truman
in commemoration of the postwar Recovery Act for Greece.

After months of gathering testimony and investigating allegations
by medical examination and other means, the commission of inquiry
concluded that there had been wholesale violation of the Human
Rights Convention in Greece. But on December 12, 1969, the Papadopoulos regime denounced the inquiry and the Council of Europe
and withdrew from it in protest. The United States sought to support
its military ally through quiet lobbying efforts by the State Department
directed at European embassies to persuade the council not to con-
demn Greece. But the efforts were to no avail. The council's findings
underline the low popularity among the Europeans of the new regime
in Greece even though it was a devoted participant in NATO. Athens
publisher Helen Vlachos, who went into exile in London after the
colonels' coup, told the House Foreign Affairs Committee in 1971
that junta-ruled Greece had become a "corpse in the ship of NATO."

"The military said the torture allegations against the junta were
trumped up, even the Council of Europe report," recalled a State

†*Ibid.*, p. 225.

Department official who took part in the NSC staff deliberations on the aid question. "The military, from the JUSMAGG mission in Athens to the Joint Chiefs in the Pentagon, were screaming, 'Turn on the aid. Is there any reason not to? None at all, except the knuckle-heads in Congress.' They pointed out that Spain and Portugal were getting our military assistance. Why shouldn't Greece?"

But the following month, September 1969, unbeknown to Congress and the public, the dilemma was resolved. The National Security Council secretly came to the conclusion that the Nixon administration should resume full-scale assistance to Greece. The decision, heavily debated within the soundproof environment of the national security bureaucracy, reflected the disposition of the new president, his Special Assistant for National Security Affairs, Henry A. Kissinger, and the Joint Chiefs of Staff. Secretary of State Rogers was reported to have been more ambivalent, since the weight of professional analytical judgment within the department leaned against resumption of aid. As the case was presented in the final NSC document that incorporated the new policy, the arguments of the military prevailed over the oft-expressed concern over the "image" of the Papadopoulos regime and the question of its return to constitutional government.

10. Agnew and Pappas

With the advent of the Nixon administration, there was a new political cast to relations between Athens and Washington. It was reflected in two public figures prominently associated with the new president by bonds of money and politics: Vice President Spiro T. Agnew and Greek-American industrial tycoon Thomas A. Pappas, who ran a $200 million investment empire in Greece. Pappas was widely credited in the press with having played an influential role in the selection of Agnew as Vice President. He was listed by Nixon campaign officials in 1972 as having been among the biggest contributors to the Republican presidential campaign—those who donated $100,000 or more. Furthermore, he was a vice president of the Committee to Re-elect the President and Nixon's principal money-raiser in Athens. In June 1970, Pappas hosted a dinner for Nixon's brother, Donald, which was attended by some leading members of the regime, including Deputy Premier Pattakos. And during that Athens trip, the President's brother consummated a deal with Aristotle Onassis for in-flight catering service on the shipowner's Olympic Airways by Marriott Corporation, of which Donald Nixon was a vice president. Pappas was called back from Greece to appear before New York authorities in the conspiracy and perjury case against former Attorney General John N. Mitchell, former Commerce Secretary Maurice Stans, and fugitive millionaire Robert L. Vesco. In Washington, Pappas was named by the Watergate Special Prosecutor's staff as one of the subjects figuring in its investigation of illegal contributions by foreign principals. However, Pappas was not criminally implicated in either proceeding.

The following year, Pappas was again the host for a visit by Stans that was given banner headline treatment in the Athens press and reported as a political benediction by the Nixon administration on the Papadopoulos regime. Stans read a message from Nixon praising Greece for its rapid economic progress under the rule of Papadopoulos. "We in the United States Government, particularly in American business, greatly appreciate Greece's attitude toward American investment, and we appreciate the welcome that is given here to American companies and the sense of security that the Government of Greece is imparting to them," Stans told a luncheon audience. The Greek newspapers also gave prominence to a Greek government communiqué quoting Stans as saying that he was asked by President Nixon to "convey to the Government of Greece and the Greek people his warm love." The American embassy, besieged by the press, issued a clarifying statement that Stans had used the words "warmth and confidence," not "warm love."

The disclosure that the Pappas foundations were used as conduits for CIA money in 1967, and his cordial relations with the junta, seemed further confirmation of the Greek Left's conviction that the CIA and American business interests were in league in Greece.

Less than a month into the 1968 presidential campaign, Agnew felt the call to speak up for the Greek junta, notwithstanding the official U.S. government policy at the time of not applauding the colonels —at least not in public. In response to a question, the GOP vice-presidential candidate said, "I think the Greek military government that took over in 1967 has not proven itself to be as horrendous a specter to contemplate as most people thought it would. . . . They have, for example, encouraged the return of Greek ship-building interests, which is one of the most important economic factors in the country." He took a heavy cut at Andreas Papandreou, saying that he was in command of "the Communist forces" in Greece, an observation that gave the voters a foretaste of Agnew's famous knack for broad-brush political characterization: "I think we have got to believe that although we don't want a military government, we look for the return of a free elective system in the tradition of Greece, that this particular military government has done a bit to stabilize the Communist threat in Greece."*

Although Henry Kissinger privately insisted that he sought to keep Agnew out of Greece, it was not long after the election that the Vice President succumbed to the temptation to return to the land of his fathers, where he heaped more praise on the regime. If the official U.S. policy was one of cool disapproval of the military government, there was little evidence of it in official American behavior.

*Clogg and Yannopoulos, *op. cit.*, p. 245.

11. The New Proconsul

In September 1969, at about the time the decision had been made within the National Security Council to resume full-scale military aid, President Nixon chose Henry J. Tasca as the new ambassador to Greece. Tasca was a career diplomat, a small man of somewhat pompous manner, with a reputation, nonetheless, for carrying out his instructions. He had treated Nixon with memorable ceremony during a visit to Morocco, where Tasca had been ambassador not long before the 1968 campaign.

The post had remained vacant for some eight months while senators and representatives pushed their respective candidates for the job. Tasca was up for reassignment, and although he had his heart set on Rome, where his wealthy Italian in-laws lived, he accepted the Athens assignment with good cheer. In Greece, Tasca's subordinates in the embassy quickly perceived what some of them described as a "special relationship" between Tasca and Richard Nixon.

Several days before the NSC meeting at which the decision was formally reached to resume aid to Greece, Tasca met with President Nixon. According to a party to the exchange, the President told the ambassador-designate of the administration's intention to restore military aid and counseled him to work amicably with Papadopoulos. The gist of Nixon's instructions, as interpreted by Tasca, was: "We've got to restore military aid; as far as the *rest* is concerned [by which Tasca understood Nixon to be alluding to Greece's constitutional future], make it look as good as you can—but the priority is military assistance." During the first few months of Tasca's tenure, Papadopoulos sent a letter to President Nixon indicating that he would return the government of Greece to constitutional order after drafting a new constitution, all to take place by the end of 1970.

After voting its confirmation of Tasca's appointment in December, the Senate Foreign Relations Committee inserted in the foreign aid authorization bill a ban on aid to Greece. The provision was swiftly defeated, however, in the Senate. What was finally passed was a sense-of-the-Senate resolution calling on the Nixon administration "to exert all possible efforts to influence a speedy return to constitutional government in Greece." What the Senate had done, with whimsical legislative logic, was to endorse a political policy toward Greece while rejecting the most practical means of achieving it. The Nixon administration meanwhile assured Congress that the new regime had every intention of restoring democratic institutions in Greece on a reasonable timetable. It was a note that State Department witnesses would sound at appropriations time year in and year out.

Tasca, in carrying out the direct mandate from Nixon, set out to establish a warm rapport with Papadopoulos. At the same time, he expressed privately to members of his staff the hope that he could use his personal leverage with the junta to encourage it back toward some form of constitutional government.

"We have two policies toward Greece," he told one political officer shortly after his arrival. "One is Nixon's and the other is Secretary of State Rogers'. I work for Nixon. I am his personal representative and I am going to carry out his policies."

"In that case," the subordinate later remembered blurting, "you are going to fail."

Tasca gave the young official a lecture. He explained that a diplomat must find the bases of power in whatever country he works and cultivate them. In Greece, it was Papadopoulos and his cronies who were in power. He would work with them and, as he put it, "bring them along without criticizing them publicly."

In the first two years of his ambassadorship, Tasca applied that precept with fervor. On Christmas Eve, American schoolchildren serenaded the junta leader in his office. There was a constant and growing procession of American VIPs, such as Stans, Agnew, Laird,

Goodpaster—all projecting a smiling face of approval from Washington.

In September 1970—nine months after Tasca had become ambassador and a full year after the decision had been made—the Nixon administration publicly announced that full-scale military aid would be resumed. The first word of the 1969 decision did not leak out to the press until May 1970, and then in a somewhat garbled form. It was a story that appeared in the *Washington Post* on May 14, 1970:

> The American ambassador to Athens, Henry J. Tasca, has recommended resuming American shipments of heavy arms to Greece, it was learned yesterday.
> Officials confirmed that Tasca has urged ending the three year boycott on tanks, planes and heavy artillery to the Greek Army.
> The boycott has been in effect since a junta of colonels overthrew Greece's parliamentary government and seized power in April, 1967. No final decision has been made on Tasca's recommendation and none is expected for at least several weeks. Ultimately the issue will be reviewed in the National Security Council and decided by President Nixon. . . .

Although it was the first substantive news account of a change in American military aid policy toward Greece, the story was garbled because official American embassy sources had lied to the reporter. Tasca was portrayed as the initiator of the request rather than as the agent of a decision made at the presidential level with concurring NSC action eight months earlier.

At the time, Tasca encouraged the notion that he was instrumental in the military aid decision. During a House Foreign Affairs European Subcommittee hearing on August 3, 1971, the chairman, Congressman Benjamin Rosenthal, asked Tasca whether at the time of his arrival the U.S. government had decided to renew military assistance.

The ambassador murkily responded, "At the time of my arrival the government had clearly understood that the importance of the security interests of the United States in that part of the world made necessary an imminent and urgent review of the problem of resuming military assistance as soon as possible."

Rosenthal patiently restated the question seven times, and each time Tasca evaded it, finally telling the congressman, "I have nothing further to add to what I have said." Long after his separation from the State Department, Tasca would acknowledge to former associates not only that the NSC decision had been made prior to his appointment but that it was wrong to have excluded him from the original decision on aid. By attributing the decision to Tasca, the State Department may have been trying to float a trial balloon for congressional reaction.

The liberals in Congress did, of course, react. A move was launched in the next session to cut off military aid. It took the form of an amendment by Congressman Wayne Hays (D-Ohio) that would have required a written presidential determination of overriding national security interest before aid could be extended to Greece. It passed in the House on August 3, 1971, the first legislative sanction imposed by either house against the Greek dictatorship. Intensive lobbying by the administration, however, contributed heavily to the defeat of the Hays amendment in the Senate. In the ensuing presidential campaign, the issue of the dictatorship in Greece scarcely occupied the attention of the candidates on either side.

The announcement of resumption of aid on September 22, 1970, was cast in classic bureaucratese. Heavy arms shipments, it said, would start again in order to "enhance the ability of the Greek forces to carry out their responsibilities in defense of the NATO area" and because "Greece offers strategic advantages to the NATO alliance and to the United States which are of great importance to the security of the West." It added, "The decision to resume shipments of suspended items rests entirely on those considerations." As an afterthought, the announcement said, "Although the United States had hoped for a more rapid return to representative government in Greece, the trend toward a constitutional order is established."

In fact, the evidence from Greece supported a completely contrary reading of the regime's intentions. Although Papadopoulos was making conciliatory noises and hinting at the probability that true constitutional government would return to Greece by the end of 1970, he publicly reneged on the promise. In December of that year, he made a speech renouncing the possibility of a change in the regime. Meanwhile, there would be no elections, and the King would have to remain in exile. He and only he would decide when the propitious moment would come for any relaxation in military rule, Papadopoulos said. For Tasca, it was the first step in a process of disenchantment that would, after four more years, turn him into a bitter and discredited victim of his own illusions and the policies he served.

The first salvo aimed at his conduct of his ambassadorial role was a confidential staff report of the House Foreign Affairs Subcommittee, compiled by staff consultant Clifford P. Hackett, which was never made public but which leaked to the English-language *Athens Daily News* and circulated to interested members of Congress. After a visit to Greece during the August recess, Hackett returned with some gloomy conclusions.

Writing of the temper of the American embassy in Athens, Hackett reported that:

> morale is very low. It seems tied to the limited possibilities for adjusting American policies to the political realities in Greece as long as the present ambassador stays in Athens. Athens is seen as a very undesirable post (despite its amenities) where assignment means service under an ambassador who has seriously erred in his perceptions of political developments and where political reporting would be subordinated to the exigencies of rescuing that ambassador and his career from those errors.
>
> The political reporting has in the judgement of several embassy officers been tailored to fit the present ambassador's preconceptions of what he hoped would be a trend toward constitutional government. The important distinction between political reporting and policy management was blurred under the ambassador's personal direction. The euphoria of Ambassador Tasca's early months in Athens . . . has now turned to a premonition of disaster, both personal and political, for the American representatives in Athens.

In Athens after Tasca's departure four years later, the same criticism could be heard from embassy staff members. Tasca, they said, intruded himself into the political reporting process—busying himself with such matters as the size of crowds at political gatherings, voicing popular approval of the military government, and downgrading the reports of repression of opponents. "He told Washington what he thought Washington wanted to hear," one of his political officers later said.

At the beginning of his tenure, Tasca portrayed himself as an ambassador in complete accord with the policy in Washington. After he was brought back from Greece without reappointment, Tasca bitterly acknowledged that he had been following orders in courting the military leadership. Yet he clung to the hope that the Papadopoulos government would finally make good its promise to prepare the way for elections and an end to rule by martial law—although with steadily growing skepticism.

Hardly had the reversal of policy on delivery of heavy weapons to Greece been announced when a new and major bond of military involvement with the junta began to take root in the American Pentagon. It was the Athens home-port plan, the brainchild of Chief of Naval Operations Elmo Zumwalt. A new Mediterranean carrier task force home-port, as he conceived it, would answer some of the U.S. Navy's most pressing needs of the day: cutting operating costs while at the same time permitting the navy to meet its global commitments, retaining existing manpower, and attracting new career recruits. The attraction from a manpower standpoint was that the overseas home-port would reduce the time married personnel would be away from their families. And if a man were single, the attractions of the Athens port city of Piraeus had been well advertised by Melina Mercouri in the film *Never on Sunday.*

The main ingredients of the home-port plan, together with the designation of Athens as the preferred site, were put together almost entirely within the confines of the Department of the Navy and delivered to the rest of the government as a bureaucratic *fait accompli.* At the Department of State, whose concurrence was needed in order to put the home-port plan into effect, there was, indeed, concurrence —but based almost entirely on the data supplied by the navy's experts. The symbolic endorsement of the regime through establishment of a major fleet headquarters in Athens apparently concerned no one at the top level of the State Department, although strong dismay was registered by the department's Greek specialists at the policy-desk level. When State Department witnesses presented the institutional view on Capitol Hill, they made clear that the policy priority in the home-port issue was the military one. In this spirit, Assistant Secretary of State Rodger Davies told the House Foreign Affairs European Subcommittee on March 8, 1972: "Our motive in establishing a home-port in Greece is clear—to improve the living conditions and morale of American servicemen, thereby allowing the Sixth Fleet to meet its commitments in the Mediterranean within stringent budgetary limits." Davies went on to say that "homeporting will undoubtedly be regarded by certain elements within Greece as a further indication of United States support and approbation of this particular regime." Davies, who was killed more than two years later in Cyprus, testified that opposition to the home-porting plan "would be restricted in the main to some elements of the former political leadership, and the political, professional, perhaps artistic elite who in the main accept the false assumption that the United States had such influence in Greece that it could bring about a change of government and maintain a government in power. This is in fact not so."

The brutal truth of the matter was propounded by another witness, Deputy Assistant Secretary Russell Fessenden, who insisted that the State Department did take into account "the constitutional government situation." But, Fessenden said:

> I don't think it would be entirely honest of me if I were to say that that was the overriding concern in all of our policy toward Europe and the Near East. It is a factor which we must take into account in an affair like this one . . . but not one that is so great that it would dominate and overrule some of the more basic concerns we have about maintaining the strength of NATO, maintaining an adequate NATO and U.S. posture in the Middle East and so forth.

Had it not been for Rosenthal's European Subcommittee and the misgivings of middle-level analysts in the Navy Department as well as the State Department, the home-port plan would have slid through the Executive Department with little more than a few downstairs murmurs. As it was, the home-port project, which was to more than double the aggregate American military presence in Athens by adding 10,000 naval personnel and dependents, sped from conception to execution with impressive bureaucratic momentum.

On September 21, 1971, the navy made its official request to the Pentagon for the carrier task force home-port in Athens. A month later, the Defense Department approved. By December 30, the State Department gave its blessings to the proposal and so notified the president. On January 20, 1972, the U.S. embassy in Athens reported the approval of the government of Greece. On May 6, 1972, the Hellenic navy approved the home-porting of the destroyer squadron (Stage One of the plan) in Athens. And finally, at 7:00 A.M. on September 1, 1972, six American destroyers cruised into Phaleron Bay, Athens, and prepared to drop anchor.

In a report on its first round of home port hearings (April 1972), the European Affairs Subcommittee reached this, among other conclusions:

> We consider the danger of pre-eminence of military and strategic considerations over political values a fundamental problem of American foreign policy decision making today. We think this homeporting decision is a good example of this disturbing trend. The subcommittee understands fully that strategic considerations are important in formulating foreign policy goals and programs, but we are convinced that strategic and military interests are ultimately jeopardized by minimizing the political consequences of decisions like homeporting in Greece.

The subcommittee, headed by Congressman Ben Rosenthal (D-New York) was admittedly an adversary forum to the Nixon administration's policies on the Greek dictatorship. It was also a sounding board for those "elements of the former political leadership" of which Davies had spoken so disparagingly in his testimony. Those very same "elements of the former leadership" returned to power in 1974 after the junta launched its suicidal coup against Makarios, which led to the death of Davies. One of the earliest actions of the same "former leadership" after returning to power was to negotiate the closing down of the home-port base for the six American destroyers in Athens. For the returned Greek democrats, it was a repugnant symbol of American collusion with the dictatorship.

PART II

12. "We Will Avenge You, Dighenis!"

The late-January rain pelted the crowd gathered in a suburban field in the Cypriot city of Limassol, turning the soil underfoot to mud. Nonetheless, the crowd kept thickening silently until some 100,000 Greek Cypriots spread outward from the open coffin of General George Grivas, the brilliant and fanatic guerrilla fighter. Fifteen years earlier, Grivas, under the mythological nom de guerre "Dighenis," had humbled the British by leading a holy war of terrorism to unite his native Cyprus with the Greek motherland. Now they came to honor his memory and bury his remains.

Hard-faced terrorists in old military uniforms, simple peasant families with black armbands of mourning, two defrocked bishops of the Byzantine church, a scattering of local and foreign journalists, the ambassador of the Greek military junta in Athens, uniformed Greek officers—but mainly the Greek-Cypriot villagers—comprised the ring upon ring of mourners who gathered around the casket. Throughout the island republic, flags were at half-mast. Schools and other public buildings were closed.

Yet, the official Cypriot government headed by President Makarios was not represented at the funeral. Grivas and his followers had come to regard Makarios as a traitor to the cause of *enosis* (union with Greece), in the aftermath of the war against the British. Makarios, in the eyes of Grivas, had betrayed the sacrifices of his heroic freedom fighters by succumbing—even though reluctantly—to the great powers in 1959 and accepting independence for Cyprus rather than *enosis*, for which they had fought. During the guerrilla campaign of the late 1950s, Grivas had personally marked men for summary execution who he felt had betrayed the cause.

On this overcast day—January 29, 1974—Makarios remained at the presidential palace in Nicosia. He knew what depths of nostalgia and pride the name of Grivas stirred in Greek-Cypriot hearts and tacitly agreed that the day of the funeral should be a day of national mourning.

Fifteen, twenty years earlier, the bombs and bullets of Grivas's guerrilla fighters had sounded the alarm against the British and emblazoned the cause of the insurgent Greeks upon the front pages of the world press and in the chambers of the United Nations. More recently, the bullets had been aimed by some of the same guerrilla cadre at Makarios in a series of assassination attempts instigated by the military rulers of Athens and their agents on Cyprus.

The colonels in Athens thought of Grivas as an important instrument in their goal of liquidating Makarios, ending the island's political autonomy, and finally achieving *enosis*. But Grivas, seventy-three years of age at the time of his death, was senior to them all in military stature—a power unto himself. Rumor had it that the actual assassination of Makarios was something to which Grivas was opposed. He and the Archbishop had once been allied in the underground struggle for *enosis*. Grivas, in the days of the insurrection, had also supported Makarios as the leader of the Greek Cypriots. But there is no doubt that Grivas and EOKA-B (National Organization of Cypriot Fighters), the underground organization he reestablished after returning to Cyprus in 1971 from house arrest in Greece, conspired with Athens to remove Makarios from power.

The funeral turned into a political underground rally, a dark celebration of Hellenic fervor by the right-wing militants who regarded Archbishop Makarios with the same suspicious hatred as did the colonels in Athens. They thought of him as a red priest who flirted with the local Communist party, AKEL (Party for Raising Up the Working People), and curried the favor of the Communist powers abroad in Moscow, Eastern Europe, and Peking.

At the casket of Grivas, the Orthodox church was represented by the three bishops, Genadios of Paphos, Anthimos of Kition, and Kyprianos of Kyrenia, who had staged an unsuccessful ecclesiastical power play to force the resignation of Makarios as President of Cyprus. They argued that it was improper for him to serve as head of both state and church. Makarios adroitly maneuvered his way out of the crisis and finally turned the tables on them by convening a synod at which the three bishops were defrocked.

But the oratorical centerpiece of the funeral was provided by Nikos Sampson, an erratic and politically ambitious newspaper publisher who had established a reputation for himself during EOKA-B days as a sadistic killer of Turks and Britons. Stories of Sampson's murderous excesses as a leader of Greek-Cypriot execution squads under Grivas are rife in Cyprus. In the Turkish enclaves, his name was a household synonym for terror. The British folklore had it that in the days during the insurrection, when Sampson was acting as a news photographer, his pictorial scoops of murdered British soldiers and policemen stemmed from the fact that he used his gun before focusing his camera. In 1957, he was sent to Britain to serve a life sentence for the murder of a British policeman, along with other members of the underground EOKA-B organization. The signing of the peace settlement in 1959 won Sampson an amnesty, and he returned to Cyprus as something of a revolutionary celebrity.

At the funeral of Grivas, Sampson arranged his personal claque of bully boys around the casket of Grivas, and as he ascended the platform to speak, his torso wrapped in a Greek flag, they shouted and applauded.

The heavyset gunman of the EOKA-B days unleased a tirade of tearful oratory and exhorted the crowd to fight for *enosis*, which had been abandoned by the double-dealing Makarios. Before mounting the platform for his scene-stealing performance, Sampson had stuffed a copy of his newspaper, *Maki* ("combat"), into the coffin with the body of Grivas. At the high point of his speech, Sampson slammed his fist on the base of the casket and screamed, "We will avenge you, Dighenis!" A solemn national rite had been turned into a one-man political rally, and many onlookers went away with a sour taste in their mouth for the entire affair.

That funeral rally was to become a green light for a new assault on Makarios by the regime in Athens and its agents in Cyprus—"Operation Aphrodite."

13. The True Minority

In the Cyprus tragedy, there were no certifiable heroes, and it is almost impossible to pinpoint the time at which original sin was committed. For nearly five years, the military rulers in Athens had been scheming to kill the Archbishop and establish their hegemony on the island. The deadly game of provocation and counterprovocation between Archbishop Makarios and his enemies, both in Cyprus and on the mainland, was played out in an atmosphere of Byzantine maneuvering that is probably unique to the island.

Before that, there were schemes by outside powers, including the United States, designed to end the recurrent troubles of Cyprus by partition and double *enosis*, with the two Aegean rivals, Greece and Turkey, sharing dominion over Cyprus. Even earlier, there were the injustices and political miscalculations by the Greek Cypriots, Grivas, as well as Makarios and his followers, directed at the Turkish population of Cyprus. Though the Turks comprised only 18 percent of the island's population, it was the Greek Cypriots who constituted the true minority in their corner of the Mediterranean. A glance at the map shows that Cyprus lies in the shadow of the Anatolian peninsula, the jumping-off point for a Turkish military machine that could easily devastate the Greek Cypriots and any mainland Greek expeditionary force that crossed the Mediterranean to do battle there.

During the *enosis* struggle, which began in earnest with the opening of Grivas's terrorism campaign in 1955, the old guerrilla fighter and the Archbishop maintained a tenuous alliance hedged with mutual suspicions. From the beginning, Makarios was dubious about the tactics of terrorism that Grivas pursued with such fanatic zest. But Makarios went along with the guerrilla campaign on the grounds that it strengthened his bargaining hand with the British. Throughout the campaign, Makarios stayed in touch with Grivas through a network of secret intermediaries. The British had put a bounty on Grivas's head, but Grivas moved successfully from house to house and from one mountain hideaway to the other, protected by his partisans. Finally, when the makeshift London-Zurich agreements were signed in 1959, conferring on Cyprus independence rather than *enosis*, Grivas left Cyprus a bitter man despite the hero's welcome that awaited him in Greece.

"I did my duty, as I saw it, to the end," Grivas concluded in his memoirs. "But the Cypriot people, who fought so bravely and for so long, deserved a better fate than the shackles which were forged for them in Zurich."*

Grivas was one of those bigger-than-life figures, men of uncompromising mission, who fall near the boundary between hero and crackpot. Grivas was a guerrilla who refused to switch from the tactic of struggle to the tactic of compromise at the time Makarios thought to be appropriate. From the signing of the London-Zurich agreement establishing the sovereignty of Cyprus, its leader, Makarios, pursued a diplomacy that had to balance off all the contending interests surrounding the island: East and West, Christian and Muslim, and above all, Greek and Turk. The governing political realities for Makarios were the Turkish colossus lying forty miles off the northern shore and the movement for the union of Cyprus and motherland, which obsessed the Greek enosists, such as Grivas, and pushed events toward collision between the two countries.

When Makarios sensed pressures from the West, or from Greece and Turkey, toward partition of the island and division of the new state he headed, he opened initiatives toward Moscow. The Soviet Union, he knew, had a strong interest in keeping Cyprus out of the NATO orbit and was content with the general policy of nonalignment followed by Makarios. Makarios also played the Third World theme in the United Nations, appealing to the growing bloc of "nonaligned"

*Memoirs of General Grivas. New York: Praeger, 1965, p. 203.

votes to champion the cause of his government's sovereignty. These tactics earned him a reputation in Washington and other Western capitals as a Communist sympathizer, a "Castro of the Mediterranean." But this was a piece of simplistic caricature. Makarios, a traditionalist and political conservative at heart, was practicing tactics of Byzantine balance-of-power governance that predated Prince Metternich and Henry Kissinger by nearly 1,500 years.

The Cypriot state that was forged out of the violence of the guerrilla war led by Grivas was a piece of diplomatic and constitutional patchwork concocted under the gun. It was a government headed by a Greek President elected by the Greek majority, which comprised 80 percent of the population. To assuage the Turks, the authors of the agreement assigned the vice presidency to a Turkish Cypriot and conferred upon him, as well as the President, the power of veto over actions of the Council of Ministers and enactments of the legislature. The framers of the constitution tried to balance the conflicts between the two ethnic communities by giving the Greeks the majority position in the government and providing the Turks with the negative equalizer of the veto. It was a formula that was regarded by the Greek Cypriots as at best a mean compromise and at worst a sellout of the objective of *enosis*.

Within three years, the result was government paralysis. Makarios, his patience at an end, sought to resolve the impasse through a series of major alterations in the constitution, chiefly, the elimination of the presidential and vice-presidential veto. The issue over which conflict had emerged most sharply was the question of maintaining separate Greek and Turkish municipalities in the five largest towns, which the Turks had insisted upon and which the Greeks in the administration considered to be costly and inefficient. The changes proposed by Makarios were rejected by the Turkish government as well as by Turkish Vice President Fadil Kutchuk. The final steps to full-scale confrontation were taken in December 1963.

The ensuing months saw the United States enter as the principal diplomatic broker and power figure in the East Mediterranean, replacing the vacuum left by the British. Turkey was on the verge of a full-scale war with Greece after a series of attacks on Turkish-Cypriot villages by Greek forces and skirmishes between both military forces, including aerial attacks by Turkish fighter-bombers.

On June 5, 1964, President Johnson, in a letter that the Turks found brutal by any prior standard of diplomatic communication, warned the Inonu government against any invasion of Cyprus. The American President said specifically that the use of American arms in Cyprus violated bilateral agreements between Washington and Ankara.

In addition, President Johnson wrote Inonu, a Turkish intervention in Cyprus "would lead to a military engagement between Turkish and Greek forces. . . . Adhesion to NATO, in its very essence, means that NATO countries will not wage war on each other. Germany and France have buried centuries of animosity and hostility in becoming NATO allies; nothing less can be expected from Greece and Turkey."

President Johnson also cited the possibility of a direct Soviet involvement if Turkey invaded Cyprus.

> I hope you will consider that your NATO Allies have not had a chance to consider whether they have an obligation to protect Turkey against the Soviet Union if Turkey takes a step which results in Soviet intervention without the full consent and understanding of its NATO allies.
>
> . . . I feel obligated to call to your attention in the most friendly fashion the fact that such a Turkish move could lead to the slaughter of tens of thousands of Turkish Cypriots on the Island of Cyprus. Such an action on your part would unleash the furies and there is no way by which military action on your part could be sufficiently effective to prevent the wholesale destruction of many of those whom you are trying to protect.

The 1964 Cyprus crisis brought the U.S. government—along with President Johnson's pressure on the Turks—into conflict with the Papandreou government in Greece and Makarios in Cyprus. Undersecretary of State George Ball, in the summer of 1964, sought to persuade Papandreou and Makarios, as well as Inonu, to accept a NATO peace-keeping force on the island rather than allow the issue to be brought into the multilateral arena of the United Nations, where the Russians would play a role in the settlement. For Makarios, who professed a policy of nonalignment and wanted now particularly to keep his lines open to the Russians, it would have been totally unacceptable to submit it to a NATO solution.

George Ball flew to Nicosia during his round of mediating and had what was by all accounts a fruitless and acrimonious meeting with an unyielding Makarios. Ball later told colleagues that he berated the Archbishop for his stubbornness in resisting the American overtures.

"I said, 'Your Beatitude, you can't turn this beautiful little island into your private *abattoir*,' " Ball told an acquaintance later. "I thought he would get angry, but he shook his head and said finally, 'Mr. Secretary, you are a very hard man.' " (Afterward, Ball made no secret of his unforgiving resentment of Makarios's role in 1964. During a Brookings Institution conference in 1969, Ball said in the presence of State Department colleagues, "That son of a bitch [Makarios] will have to be killed before anything happens in Cyprus.")

The American initiative was a plan devised by Special Emissary Dean Acheson to achieve a partition of Cyprus in the grand tradition of postwar diplomacy. It envisaged the union of the major territory of Cyprus with Greece. Turkey would have been ceded territory to the north, the Karpas Peninsula, as a military base. Enclaves would have been established for Turkish Cypriots who wished to stay, while compensation would be provided to those who wished to leave the island and resettle. The tiny island of Kastelorrizon, just off the Turkish coast, would be transferred to Turkey.

When Makarios learned of the Acheson blueprint, he mustered all his guile and influence to defeat it. While Papandreou privately was signaling his desire to reach a settlement and remove the Cyprus tumor from the internal politics of Greece, Makarios stood adamantly against any such solution. It would have meant his own political demotion to, at most, a provincial proconsul in both political and ecclesiastical standing.

Nonetheless, the Johnson letter and the persuasions of Ball and the rest of the Johnson administration finally induced the Turks to abandon their plans to invade. But, in the aftermath of the 1964 crisis, the Greek majority was reinforced by some 12,000 to 14,000 troops infiltrated by the Papandreou government in anticipation of a Turkish attack.

For the Greek leaders in Cyprus as well as in Athens, the lesson to be drawn from the face-down of that year was that the United States could be depended upon to intervene to prevent war within the NATO alliance. As always throughout post-Byzantine Greek history, important outcomes were decided by outsiders. Makarios had played an adroit game of balance of power, and the results of the 1964 crisis confirmed the wisdom of his approach. For the Turks, it was rude humiliation imposed by the United States, which Turkish pride would never forgive or forget.

This dissipation of the 1964 Greek-Turkish confrontation over Cyprus was not so much an end as an interlude. Within three years, the four sets of protagonists—Greek Cypriot, Turkish Cypriot, Greek, and Turk—were ready to go to war again. In Greece, the Papadopoulos junta had taken over, and Cyprus was its first foreign policy crisis.

Foolishly, Papadopoulos agreed to a meeting with his Turkish counterpart, Prime Minister Demirel, at the Evros River on the Thracian border. Papadopoulos proposed *enosis*, along with some territorial concessions for the Turks, a scheme along the lines of the American-sponsored Acheson Plan of three years earlier. The Turks scoffed at the Greek proposal and returned home. The only outcome of the meeting, which had been opposed by the Greek diplomatic professionals, was to demonstrate the dangerous naiveté and powerlessness of the new rulers in Athens.

On November 15, 1967, Grivas ordered attacks on two Turkish-Cypriot villages, Kophinou and Ayios Theodoros, with a slaughter of Turkish villagers ensuing, and by the following week, the Ankara government was poised to invade. This time, President Johnson sent Cyrus Vance, the respected Wall Street lawyer who had been his Secretary of the Army, to the East Mediterranean. There began a remarkable ten days of round-the-clock shuttle diplomacy in which Vance dealt amicably with all the principals in the conflict and worked out a solution that was, in effect, an abject surrender for the Greek regime. Vance, throughout the negotiating marathon, was afflicted with severe back pains. During his discussions with Makarios in Nicosia, the subject of Vance's backache came up and the Archbishop, a fellow sufferer, took time out from their deliberations to try on Vance's specially designed back brace. Unlike the bitter Ball-Makarios meetings of 1964, the new American envoy and the Cypriot President had a friendly and productive exchange.

Reluctantly, the colonels in Athens and Makarios in Nicosia agreed to the withdrawal of the 12,000 Greek forces infiltrated during the Papandreou administration, as well as the removal of Grivas to Greece. The two Cypriot sides also began the intercommunal talks that were intended to solve their differences at the local level.

Fundamentally, the ascent to power of the regime of the colonels on April 21, 1967, in Athens inaugurated an era of confrontation between Makarios and Greece. The new rulers of Greece regarded them-

selves as saviors of Hellenic Christianity. They saw their country succumbing to the vices of communism, cosmopolitanism, and moral de-
cay. The leaders were narrow-gauged men with undistinguished military reputations. Since, as previously mentioned, most had been members of the KYP, the new leaders were well schooled in the techniques
of intelligence and political repression by their American counterparts.
To them, Makarios was a traitor to *enosis*, a red priest who flirted with
the local Communist party, championed nonalignment, and consorted
with such dubious Third World figures as Tito of Yugoslavia and
Nasser of Egypt, not to mention his friendliness with Moscow. (Many
of them had served in the Greek officer contingent on Cyprus under
the rule of Makarios.)

In 1970, the first serious assassination attempt was launched against
the Archbishop. It centered on a hero of the EOKA guerrilla-war days,
Polycarpus Georhadjis, whose exploits against the British and espe-
cially his facility for escape earned him the title of the "Greek-Cypriot
Houdini." Georhadjis became Minister of Interior when the government of Cyprus was constituted under Makarios, and he was also
known as a compulsive keeper of "dirt" on all the major personalities
on the island. The year before the assassination conspiracy, Georhadjis and Makarios had a falling-out, and the minister was stripped of
his portfolio. He became the perfect instrument for the Greek agents
in their scheming against the Archbishop. One of the Greek officers, a
Colonel Papapostoulou, cleverly exacerbated the ragged relations between the two Cypriot leaders and then, by a combination of threats
and promises, won Georhadjis's complicity.

But somehow, word of an assassination scheme against the Archbishop was leaked to the CIA station in Nicosia. In January 1970,
during a trip by Makarios to West Africa, a member of the U.S. embassy in Nairobi insisted on conveying a private message to the Archbishop.

Makarios recalled during an interview:

> We were about to have lunch. I was late in arriving and someone
> in the American Embassy insisted that he had an urgent message.
> We were in a hurry and I was not very pleased at the interruption,
> but I agreed to hear him. The message was this: "According to re-
> liable sources, when you go back to Cyprus there are plans for your
> assassination at the airport in Nicosia."
> This was the first time I had heard of an attempt being made on

my life. I smiled and said, "Thank you very much, but I don't think
it is probable." Actually, I didn't think the airport would be a suitable place for an assassination. But the American said, "Be careful."

Nothing happened immediately although back in Nicosia in late February, Makarios was again approached, this time by U.S. Ambassador
David Popper. "He said, 'The information we conveyed to you in
Nairobi has been confirmed,'" Makarios recalled. "'The attempt on
your life will take place any time within the next fifteen days.'"

Several days later, Georhadjis phoned his successor in the Interior
Ministry, T. K. Anastosiu, and informed him of the impending move
against Makarios. Anastosiu warned against getting mixed up in the
scheme. "You will bring the country a lot of misery," the minister
told Georhadjis. "You should not carry a personal grudge this far."
Georhadjis replied, the other man later recalled: "Don't worry, the
future is with us. The Americans are behind us." Anastosiu immediately called the American embassy and reported, "They are mixing
your name up in clandestine activities." He remembered that the
Americans took the warning most seriously.

On March 8, slightly more than two weeks after Popper's warning,
Makarios was leaving the presidential palace when machine-gun fire
opened up from the roof of the nearby Hellenic Gymnasium. The
helicopter crashed and the pilot was seriously injured. Makarios
stepped off unhurt.

Afterward, he wondered publicly how the Americans had known
about the assassination attempt, which had escaped the attention of his
own intelligence service. The information had, in fact, come from CIA
covert intelligence channels, as Makarios must have known. At the
time, Makarios was deeply suspicious of the activities of Eric Neff,
the CIA Station Chief in Nicosia. Neff made no secret of his antipathy
for Makarios. The CIA official had, in fact, said openly in the tight
little diplomatic world of Nicosia that Makarios had to go. "He made
statements," one former European diplomat in Nicosia recalled, "which
would have been intolerable for any host government." Makarios also
took a dim view of Neff's contacts with Georhadjis, who worked
closely with the American CIA during his tenure as Minister of Interior, mostly on intelligence operations against external and internal
Communist targets. One high-ranking American diplomat, who was
no admirer of the former CIA official, discounted Cypriot suspicions

that Neff gave support to conspiracies against the Archbishop. But he felt strongly that Neff, a man of prepossessing personality with Harvard and Oxford training, was "too big for the island." Makarios quietly asked the American embassy to recall him, and Neff left Nicosia in 1971.

Ten days after the assassination attempt, Georhadjis, in the company of his bodyguard, drove to a secret rendezvous where he was to meet two Greek officers. The Greeks had promised to spirit him off the island to safety in Greece, Cypriot intelligence officials later learned. Georhadjis traveled the last few hundred years to his meeting on foot, leaving the bodyguard behind. Shots were heard and the bodyguard fled. Georhadjis was found shot fatally through the head, mute witness to the conspiracy. In Athens, the political section of the American embassy proposed a CIA investigation of the Georhadjis affair. But the CIA station was adamant against an investigation, it was privately acknowledged by State Department sources responsible at that time for monitoring political developments in Cyprus.

This was the bloody denouement of the first major assassination attempt on Makarios, which was inscribed in Cypriot intelligence archives as "Operation Hermes."

In September 1971, the Papadopoulos regime began to mount a new campaign to unseat the government of Makarios. Grivas escaped the loose form of house arrest by which he had been held in custody as a condition of the 1967 Cyprus settlement. Upon returning to Cyprus, Grivas reconstituted the EOKA organization of preindependence days. The new incarnation was called EOKA-B.

The regime moved this time through the church as well as the underground organization to inflame public opinion against Makarios and rekindle the struggle for *enosis*. The three bishops of the Greek orthodox church of Cyprus began agitating against Makarios, with the argument that he should not maintain a dual role as head of the church and the state, even though the concept of ethnarchy—combined temporal and spiritual leadership—was deeply engrained in Byzantine tradition. The object of the bishops' revolt was to force Makarios to surrender the presidency.

While the revolt was brewing on the clerical front, the regime moved toward open confrontation with Makarios at the political level. The justification was an attempt to import a large quantity of Czech arms for the Makarios government's police and tactical forces. The weapons were ordered by Director-General of the Ministry of Interior Anastosiu, who said in a later interview that the cache consisted mainly of Bren automatics and handguns for the police. "Our purpose," explained Anastosiu, "was to strengthen the police force in Limassol and Paphos in order to release the national guard from those places and enable the troops to move to the north in the event of a Turkish invasion."

On February 12, Papadopoulos issued a letter to Makarios, presenting him with a series of political ultimatums: he must take strong action against the Communist party; he was to form a government of "national reconciliation" that recognized Greece to be the center of Hellenism; he was to fire Foreign Minister Spyros Kyprianou, whom the regime considered too leftist and anti*enosis*. Makarios resorted to his characteristic strategy of ambivalence toward Athens, as his tactical police stamped heavily on the EOKA-B organization in Cyprus.

On February 14, during a raid on EOKA-B headquarters, the intelligence service found detailed plans for a coup that was timed to come off within twenty-four hours. Makarios, upon being informed of the find, rushed Speaker of the House Glafkos Clerides to see Ambassador Popper. As recounted by a high-ranking Cypriot officeholder who was centrally involved in the incident, Clerides told Popper that the Cypriot government had learned of the imminent coup and that the evidence intimated that the Americans were aware of it.

After Clerides briefed Popper on what he knew, the American ambassador replied with words that implanted suspicions, surviving to this day, among the Cypriot leaders: "I am not authorized to tell you anything."

Clerides, according to an authoritatively informed participant, replied bluntly: "Look, we know everything. We are going to have a coup and bloodshed."

Popper asked for time to contact Washington. His alarm was, in turn, relayed to Ambassador Henry J. Tasca in Athens, who within hours appealed to Papadopoulos not to commit any violence in Cyprus. "I warned him against any heavy stuff," Tasca later recounted in an interview, "and stressed our interest in continuation of the intercommunal talks." Makarios's security forces, in the meanwhile, struck at all the staging points for the coup. By nightfall, the Greek officer contingent on Cyprus, which had been awaiting the green light, got the definitive word from Athens: the coup was off.

The episode was prominently reported in the Cypriot press, and the United States was warmly applauded for averting armed action by the junta against Makarios. Once again, the Archbishop had been fortunate in his precarious high-wire act, in part through intervention of the United States.

In July 1972, the intelligence service of Cyprus intercepted plans for another more ambitiously scaled attempt to overthrow Makarios, this time code-named "Operation Apollo." It called for use of tank, mortar, and artillery attacks—dropping all pretensions that the assault would be conducted by the lightly armed EOKA-B forces. "The fact that heavy equipment was called for in the plans told us unmistakably that the Greek officers were involved," a senior intelligence adviser to Makarios told me. Through preemptive strikes by the government's tactical police about a week before the planned attack, as well as the publicizing of the Apollo scheme, another coup attempt was foiled by the Archbishop.

Concurrent with the hatching of the various coup schemes against Makarios, the Athens regime engaged in a series of secret contacts with the Turks to explore the possibilities for mutual action to achieve a final solution to the Cyprus problem. The colonels had a plan of partition under which a major portion of the island would revert to Greece while a part of Cyprus would come under Turkish control. The Turks would use their territorial share to establish a military presence as a protection to the Turkish-Cypriot minority against any repetitions of the 1963 or 1967 massacres.

One such meeting was conducted in Lisbon in 1971 between then Turkish Foreign Minister Olcay and Greek Foreign Minister Palamas. "Nothing was drafted, but the meetings seemed rather promising," said a high-ranking Turkish diplomat who participated in the sessions.

> There was a great effort on the part of both sides to eliminate misconceptions. We insisted that the Greeks get rid of the misconception of a unitary state in Cyprus which was foreign to the original conception of the sovereign state. The Greeks hinted indirectly that if worse came to worse, instead of breaking relations between Greece and Turkey they might be agreeable to a kind of separation, a territorial arrangement might be envisaged with a large base for Turkey so that the Turks would feel more secure. The population would be left as it was.

These secret talks were conducted first in Lisbon and later in Paris under the cover of NATO conferences. The two foreign ministers and their advisers met for what were called "bilateral lunches," held discreetly in their respective embassies. No notes were taken.

The sessions, devoted to the fate of Cyprus, were conducted behind the back of Makarios and his government. But the Archbishop was alerted to the conversations in Lisbon and Paris by his ubiquitous Chief of Intelligence, George Tombazos. The clandestine contacts were publicly denounced by Spyros Kyprianou, Foreign Minister of the Makarios government. The following year, Papadopoulos demanded Kyprianou's dismissal in his ultimatum to Makarios. This was the only demand from Athens to which the Archbishop acceded.

The attitude of the American government toward Makarios ranged from support of the London-Zurich settlement in 1959 and 1960 to a position of sour disapproval during the 1963-1964 crisis, when most U.S. foreign policy managers would have been perfectly happy to see the willful and uncooperative Cypriot President evaporate from the international scene. Following the 1967 crisis, which stemmed in large measure from a series of attacks by the Cypriot national guard then under the direction of Grivas, American policy shifted toward support for the intercommunal talks. These talks began in 1968 under the auspices of the United Nations, and their objective was to try to make the 1960 constitution work in a way that would protect Turkish minority rights and also permit the government of the republic to function. From the beginning of those talks, the public policy of the United States was to support the dialogue and deplore any thoughts of a coup in Athens against the Archbishop's government.

But there was an overriding contradiction in the U.S. position. The liquidation of Makarios became one of the fundamental objectives of Greek foreign policy under the rule of the junta, with which the United States identified itself in an ever closer and warmer embrace during the Nixon years.

14. Omens and Portents

This was the setting, thoroughly in keeping with the tradition of Byzantium, of maneuver and conspiracy surrounding the rule of Makarios in Cyprus as events marched toward the debacle of midsummer 1974.

The first omen of a new crisis was the upheaval in Athens in November 1973 that replaced the regime of Papadopoulos, which had begun to moderate its policies on domestic issues, with a new military *caudillo*—General Dimitrios Ioannides, the Chief of the Greek Military Police. An austere and reclusive figure, he had distinguished himself by the tactics of murderous brutality in the suppression of student demonstrations at Athens Polytechnic Institute in November 1973. He was an innocent in matters of government management and a primitive in politics, a man who saw Communist political devils everywhere beyond his narrow creed of Hellenic jingoism. He was, in short, everything his predecessors were—only more so.

Ioannides had once served in the Greek officer contingent on Cyprus, where he acquired an immediate and enduring antipathy for Makarios as a fellow traveler, enemy of *enosis*, and enemy of Hellenism. Makarios recalled in an interview with the Italian journalist Oriana Fallaci how Ioannides came to him one day during the 1964 intercommunal violence:

> One day he had come to see me, accompanied by Nikos Sampson. He wanted to "see me secretly to suggest to me a project that would

have settled forever the problem of Cyprus." He entered, he kissed my hand very respectfully, then: "Your Beatitude, here is my project. To attack the Turkish Cypriots suddenly, everywhere on the island, and eliminate them to the last one." I was astonished, speechless. Then I told him that I could not agree with him; I told him that I couldn't even conceive of killing so many innocents. He kissed my hand again and went away very angry.

Under Ioannides, the machinery of national administration began to disintegrate, a process hastened by a steady hemorrhage in the career civil service of those who could no longer tolerate the growing shambles to which the civilian government was being reduced. The Ioannides regime demonstrated itself to be not only more repressive than the earlier junta but even more incompetent. Ioannides regarded the public government as a ceremonial facade, a logistical base. He installed his own cronies in key positions, such as the head of the Central Intelligence Service, keeping his own title as Chief of Military Police. In the Papadopoulos regime, the Chief of Intelligence, Michael Roufogalis, had been an archrival and, when Ioannides came to power, Roufogalis was not only cast out of office but also, according to recent accounts, arrested and tortured. Under Ioannides, in other words, the seven-year military dictatorship in Greece was on its final slide toward self-destruction.

The second omen was the death of Grivas in January 1974. Grivas had an independent base of power of Cyprus and, rumor had it, had become an irritation to Athens coup planners. Grivas's handpicked successor to head the EOKA-B movement, Major George Karousas, was advocating a turning away from military terror tactics toward a more political approach to the crusade for *enosis*. He incurred the displeasure of the EOKA-B hotheads and, more important, of the Greek military coup plotters in Nicosia and at the Greek Pentagon in Athens.

One night early in April, while Makarios's intelligence officials watched in silence, Karousas was spirited off the island in a small boat. The head of the Cyprus Central Information Agency, Tombazos, was observing from a small plane overhead as Karousas was then transferred to a yacht. When he was deposited on the small Greek island of Kastelorrizon, Makarios's agents were watching the operation clandestinely from the nearby Turkish shore. The object of the intensive stakeout was to determine whether or by whom Karousas would be replaced as head of the EOKA-B forces. But no replacement appeared. As events would later demonstrate, the strings of leadership were now being pulled directly from Athens, five hundred miles away.

Early in 1974, Cyprus's Ambassador to the United States, Nikos Dimitriu, had a visitor in his Washington embassy who had just come from the island and carried a message from intelligence officials of the Makarios government. What Dimitriu heard impelled him to seek out then Assistant Secretary of State for Near Eastern Affairs Rodger Davies and Cyprus Country Director Thomas Boyatt at the State Department. "I have reliable intelligence estimates," the usually calm ambassador told Davies "that a serious effort will be made to assassinate Archbishop Makarios before Greek Easter." In Nicosia, the slogan was already making the rounds of EOKA-B circles that "Makarios will never eat his *flaouna*" (a Greek Easter confection).

"If you have a coup in Cyprus," Dimitriu told the two State Department officials, "it will develop into a crisis of gigantic dimensions. The Turks will move in and God knows where it will lead." Davies replied that the Americans had also heard rumors of an impending coup but were able to confirm nothing. Boyatt shared Dimitriu's apprehensions on the basis of his own reading of the cables and his three years of experience in Cyprus as a U.S. political officer. Several days later, Dimitriu encountered British Ambassador Sir Peter Ramsbotham, himself a former ambassador to Cyprus. He recounted his concerns to his British friend. Ramsbotham acknowledged that his country's intelligence service had heard similar things but concluded the reports were "quite groundless."

In Athens, U.S. Ambassador Henry Tasca also pooh-poohed the coup rumors. Tasca shared the view that prevailed in higher precincts of the department that Boyatt was a mother hen who needlessly worried his colleagues in Washington and Athens with dire predictions of coups against Makarios.

Greek Easter came and went without a coup, reinforcing the remark heard on the seventh floor of the State Department that the Cyprus specialists had predicted three hundred of the last two coup attempts against Makarios.

To the extent that high-level officials of the State Department were concerned with Aegean matters, their attention was focused on the belligerent growls between Greece and Turkey over oil exploration rights in the Aegean Sea. "If there was any danger of war," recalled one senior policymaker, "we felt at the time that it was over oil and not Cyprus."

Nevertheless, the nervousness in Nicosia grew. As an illustration, Glafkos Clerides came to the American embassy with a report from his government's intelligence service that Eric Neff, the former CIA Station Chief who had aligned himself openly against Makarios during his tenure in Nicosia, had been spotted in Athens. Neff, the report held, had consulted there with Sampson and EOKA-B figures. The State Department queried the CIA and received assurances that Neff had not been in Athens. The Cypriot officials then provided more specific details, including the date, February 12, of Neff's alleged presence in Athens. Further checking revealed that the former agent had, indeed, been in Athens, but the CIA insisted that he had made no contact with Sampson or the EOKA-B movement. Some Cypriot officials accepted the explanation. Others remained skeptical. The Neff episode, needless to say, fed suspicions in Cyprus of CIA implication in the coup. There were other unsettling reports, one of which found its way into print in the *New York Times* on August 2, 1974, saying that a veteran Greek-American CIA operative, Peter Koromilas, had conferred with Ioannides shortly before the July 15 coup. But this report was denied by the Athens Station Chief, Stacy Hults, even to high-ranking officials of the American embassy in Athens.

By spring 1974, signs of military, logistical, and financial preparations for another coup attempt were becoming clearer and clearer. The intelligence service of Makarios had, in a raid on an EOKA-B hideaway, founds records indicating that the organization's arms smuggling and other operations had been running at a rate of $6,000 a day starting in mid-1972. A Greek shipowner and playboy political conspirator named Andres Potamyanos was one of the chief financing "angels" in Athens, although his own net worth would not have supported so lavish a scale of expenditures. On the island, businessman Socrates Iliades, a former lieutenant of Grivas's in the first EOKA phase, had resumed his former role as a smuggler of arms to the underground organization. To anyone who could read the subsurface signs, there was a strong sense of *déjà vu* on the island, recalling the spirit of the anti-British resistance during the 1950s. Only this time, the target was not the British governor. It was Archbishop Makarios.

From Nicosia, the American embassy was reporting growing tension between Makarios and the 6,000-member national guard. The guard was the only real army in Cyprus and it was commanded from Athens. The Chief of Staff of the guard, Colonel Papadakis, was openly allied with the EOKA-B forces and the Greek officer contingent. There was a series of staged raids by EOKA-B forces on national guard arsenals, weapons lootings that in the eyes of Cypriot intelligence suggested collusion between the two organizations.

Makarios, who read the ominous implications in what was happening, sought by various strategems to gain control over the national guard. He insisted that he be given authority to appoint to the guard cadets whose loyalty was more reliable than the loyalty of those selected by the mainland officers. He asked that the size of the guard be reduced, and he also conducted a campaign to have Athens recall the Greek officers and replace them with Cypriots. Athens spurned the requests.

15. Battle of the Cables

At the State Department in Washington, the incoming cables from Nicosia seem to have stirred only the specialist in the area. At the same time, with remarkably maladroit timing, Kissinger conducted a major bureaucratic reshuffle of the Greek, Cyprus, and Turkish policy desks in April and May 1974, transferring them from the Office of Near East Affairs to the Office of European Affairs, headed by Arthur Hartman and his deputy, Wells Stabler, neither of whom had any particular experience in East Mediterranean affairs. Though there was some logic in the geographic rearrangement, it could not have come at a worse time.

The responsiveness of bureaucracy to crisis situations depends to a large extent on the knit of personal relationships and mutual trusts that build up over a period of time. "For us, Hartman and Stabler were 'new boys' in the desk organization," recalled one bureaucratic participant in the administrative shuffle. "There were difficulties in communication. They didn't know or trust us, and the feeling was reciprocal. Those first days were very tough."

One of the most insistent pleaders at the working level for high-level attention to the newly inflamed situation on the island was Boyatt, a career foreign service officer who had himself served on Cyprus during the crisis-ridden years. Outspoken by nature and convinced by professional judgment that Makarios was still the most constructive influence on the island from the standpoint of its own long-term stability as well as U.S. interests, Boyatt issued a series of warning cables upward through the policy bureaucracy.

In a mid-May cable to his superiors, the gist of which was obtained through independent sources, Boyatt pointed to the fundamental and dangerous political contradiction in Athens. The State Department classified this cable traffic and refused to make it available on grounds of national security. Boyatt told his superiors what every American political officer in the Athens embassy knew: The formal government of Greece, namely, the Foreign Ministry and civilian leadership, was issuing statements supporting the intercommunal talks, peaceful resolution of differences, cooperation with Turkey, and opposing violence. Yet, Greece's invisible government, the military junta commanded by Ioannides, was instructing the Greek army officers in Cyprus to conspire with EOKA-B to overturn Makarios and adopt the cause of *enosis.* The cable closed with a strong recommendation that the American ambassador in Athens personally tell Ioannides to abandon the plans for a coup.

Tasca balked. He responded from Athens that he had a lot of other issues on the griddle, such as renegotiation of American base rights in Greece. He did not want to meddle in the internal affairs of the Greek government. Furthermore, the ambassador wired back, unidentified sources in Athens reported that the Greek military forces in Cyprus were being brought under control. This was a piece of unintended irony. The Greek forces were indeed being brought "under control" but to carry out the very scheme of violence against which Tasca was issuing his hollow admonitions in Athens.

Tasca's reply drew another cable from the Cyprus Country Director. The views of Athens were appreciated, Boyatt's draft document said. Yet, for a number of years, the Greek military had clung to the notion that Makarios was a red priest and that Cyprus was a Mediterranean Cuba. The Greek military still expressed a strong emotional commitment to *enosis.* Turkey was also regarded as the sworn hereditary enemy. This position, the document continued, was fraught with danger and impelled the junta toward actions that were dangerous to all parties to the dispute.

This important analytical document, which was also stamped with the seal of secrecy by the State Department, recited the involvement of the Greek military in the 1970 attempted helicopter assassination of Makarios and the junta's duplicity in letting Grivas slip back into

Cyprus in November 1971, as well as its scheming to depose him through such political ruses as the bishops' revolt in 1972.

The junta, Boyatt pointed out, had a consistent record for years of supporting anti-Makarios and pro-*enosis* elements on the island. There was no evidence, the draft insisted, that the Greek government was trying to control its troops in Cyprus. In fact, the evidence was just to the contrary: The government was encouraging anti-Makarios activity by its troops.

Boyatt went on to warn that if Cyprus became embroiled in war, it was not an internal affair but rather a full-scale international debacle that would bring two NATO allies to a serious military confrontation. Once again, Boyatt urged that Tasca make these points directly to the leaders of the junta government.

The indifference about Cyprus at the higher policy levels of the State Department was shattered by a CIA communication that arrived in Washington in the third week of June. Its contents were closely held at the top of the national security bureaucracy and are still classified. Based on a direct contact with Ioannides, the intelligence bulletin made it clear that the junta leader was considering a move against Makarios as a serious option to end the tensions over Cyprus once and for all. There are different accounts of the CIA communication among those in government who had access to it, some holding that it was an explicit declaration of intentions, others saying that it was more ambiguous—perhaps a testing of U.S. reaction.

According to official intelligence sources, Ioannides complained that Makarios was manipulating Greek-Turkish tensions over the Aegean Sea and Cyprus to enhance his own political position. There had been rumors in Athens about the possibility that Makarios might allow a Greek government-in-exile to form in Cyprus, catapulting the Archbishop to national leadership in the way that Sophocles Venizelos four decades earlier had used Crete as a springboard to the prime ministership in Athens. Ioannides had concluded, according to the intelligence report, that the efforts of Makarios had to be checked. Removal from office was the one sure way to achieve this. It is significant that Ioannides chose the CIA rather than normal State Department channels for his only substantive contact with Washington in the entire pre-crisis period.

Within two days, new instructions went out to Tasca, this time signed by Undersecretary of State for Political Affairs Joseph Sisco, a veteran of the 1964 Ball mission, urging that the American ambassador meet with the head of the Greek junta and warn him against any resort to violence on the island. Tasca responded equivocally, assuring Washington that he had conveyed Washington's warning "at appropriate levels." In fact, what happened in Athens was a pathetic diplomatic shadow play by Tasca and his chief staff subordinates. The ambassador made his representations to Prime Minister Admantios Androutsopoulos, a former hotel clerk and a man who literally shook in the presence of Ioannides; to the Foreign Ministry, which senior Greek diplomats were now evacuating because of their clear premonition of what lay ahead; to chiefs of the armed services, whose principal link to the American mission was through Joint United States Military Assistance Command, Greece, and the military aid program. Tens of millions of dollars of annual U.S. military aid to Greece at least guaranteed entree for the American ambassador to the Greek Pentagon even though he could get no answers there.

Washington, not satisfied with Tasca's responses, wired him again and again in late June and early July, asking for confirmation that he had actually spoken to Ioannides. Tasca was unable to provide that assurance. Ioannides was apparently accessible only to the CIA station. And Tasca finally made a point of protocol to explain his failure to see the general whose actual title was still Chief of the Military Police.

As he put it afterward in an interview with *Newsweek,* "You don't make diplomatic démarches to a cop." In this case, however, the cop was the ruler of Greece.

Although he didn't realize it at the time, the noose was being drawn in Athens and Washington around Tasca and his foreign service career. His chief political patron, President Nixon, with whom Tasca was widely believed to enjoy a "special relationship," was moving toward impeachment in the Watergate scandal. There was also a growing recognition at the top of the State Department of Tasca's powerlessness in dealing with the Greek junta, a condition that stemmed as well from the policies formulated in Washington toward the Athens regime. The American ambassador was mounting the scaffold to be hanged as the scapegoat of the State Department. Tasca found himself caught in a sudden turnabout in the policies of Kissinger and his top foreign policy managers toward the junta in Athens.

On two occasions, at the time of the Ioannides coup in November

1973 and again during a full-dress review and consultation in Washington, Kissinger had personally ordered the Athens ambassador to take a low profile in his dealings with the junta—to avoid meddling in the internal policies of the Athens regime and to give primacy to the military and national security relationships between Washington and Athens. The later, urgent cables from Washington ordering Tasca, in effect, to confront Ioannides on the Cyprus issue represented a strong departure from past instructions. Furthermore, while Tasca's superiors were leaning heavily on him to convey Washington's message in Athens, there is no evidence that any initiatives were undertaken by either Kissinger or Sisco to call in the Greek Ambassador to Washington, Constantine Panayotakos, to register the U.S. government's severe disapproval of any coup action against Makarios.

A Greek Foreign Ministry official deeply involved in the Athens side of the Cyprus crisis said in a private interview many months afterward that "if Kissinger had called in our ambassador in Washington, it would have been a valuable weapon in our hands. We could have gone screaming to the generals saying, 'Look what we are being told in Washington.' As it was, the regime considered the warnings from Tasca as window dressing and not as serious American objections to a coup."

One of Greece's most senior foreign policy officials at the time of the Cyprus crisis acknowledged in an interview that "we had absolutely no contacts with Ioannides. . . . In fact, our biggest problem was determining who ruled the government." This was the Foreign Ministry to which Tasca was addressing Washington's admonitions against any violence in Cyprus. To say that the foreign policy bureaucracy of Athens was utterly passive and ineffectual in influencing the junta would be an understatement. On July 1, 1974, the top three career officials of the Ministry of Foreign Affairs resigned in the face of what each saw as an irreversible move by the Ioannides junta toward catastrophe in Cyprus. Those resignations should have been regarded as an alarm in Washington. But the news received only scant attention in the diplomatic reports and the press. At the time, a high State Department official privately described the resignations as "routine retirements."

Even the CIA, the most reliable pipeline into the junta, wavered in its projections of the Ioannides coup intentions. On July 3, according to intelligence specialists in Washington, the CIA received a message that Ioannides had decided to abandon the coup option, suggesting that he was responding to U.S. pressures against such action.

Again, on the eve of the coup, July 14, the agency reported new evidence that Ioannides was backing off. This calming intelligence bulletin was being read by the national security establishment in Washington the next day, as the tanks of the junta were smashing their way across Cyprus and Makarios was fleeing the island. "The CIA reporting at this stage was so bad it was hard to believe," said one diplomat intimately involved in this sequence of events. "They were reporting that the Greek military junta was firmly behind Ioannides and that a Turkish invasion would solidify the Greeks behind the general. The intelligence was really screwed up."

16. *Operation Aphrodite*

It was on the day of the first CIA reassessment of the coup prospects, July 3, that Makarios, in an uncharacteristically frontal gesture, issued an audacious challenge to the junta in Athens—a gambit clearly designed to force its hand in the crisis. He directed his letter to Greek President Phaedon Ghizikis, accusing Athens of conspiring to assassinate him and overturn his government.

"It is with profound grief," Makarios wrote, "that I have to set out to you certain inadmissible situations and events in Cyprus for which I regard the Greek government as responsible." Makarios charged that it was from Athens that

> the tree of evil, the bitter fruits of which the Greek Cypriots are tasting today, is being fed and maintained and helped to grow and spread. In order to be absolutely clear, I say that the cadres of the military regime of Greece support and direct the activities of the EOKA-B terrorists. . . . It is also known, and an undeniable fact, that the opposition Cyprus press, which supports the criminal activity of EOKA-B and which has its source of financing in Athens, receives guidance and [policy] line from those in charge of the General Staff Office and the branch of the Greek Central Intelligence Agency in Cyprus.

The most chilling omen in the Makarios letter was his declaration to Ghizikis that "I have more than once so far felt, and in some cases I have touced, a hand invisibly extending from Athens and seeking to liquidate my human existence."

He demanded that the Greek officers staffing the national guard be withdrawn and announced that he was taking over control of the guard, which had become the cutting edge of the conspiracies against him.

Now the battle was joined. Makarios removed any doubts that he was engaged in anything but a full-scale confrontation with the junta he long despised by telling Ghizikis that his communication was "not confidential." While the junta pondered its response, Makarios fired additional salvos through his own partisan press in Nicosia. On July 5, the Cypriot newspaper *Apogevmatini*, fed presumably from the presidential palace, published the gist of new coup plans found by Makarios's intelligence operatives. "The conspiratorial brains," the newspaper reported, "are planning a broad coupist action to take place in the next few days supported by certain military circles in cooperation with units of the national guard and EOKA-B groups for the purpose of seizing power. This coupist action has been planned in such a way that it formally releases senior military personnel or Greek army staff circles from any responsibility."

The newspaper said that the coup scheme—"a variation of the well-known Apollo Plan"—envisaged the assassination of Makarios. "If the plan succeeds, the government will be taken over by a certain person who has already been chosen and who, in substance, will be the puppet for a transitional period. Naturally, it is understood that the partition of Cyprus will be achieved through the coup plan with the understanding that the Turks have their plans prepared for such a golden opportunity."

They were prophetic words. The coup followed to a striking degree the blueprint outlined in the newspaper, which was available on the streets of Nicosia on the morning of July 5. The following morning, the press published the full text of the Archbishop's letter to Ghizikis. Nicosia's newspaper, *Eleftheria*, said that morning, "The statement made by President Makarios yesterday proves that the hands of the crisis almost touched the zero hour and that the blowing up of all the bridges in relations between Cyprus and Greece is still impending." A Turkish radio broadcast to Cyprus said, "The disputes that have been going on in the Greek Cypriot sector for a long time have now reached a critical stage. Some observers describe the current situation as a serious crisis unprecedented in the history of Cyprus."

On July 6, according to the widely respected Athens correspondent for the *Times of London*, Mario Modiano, Ioannides and his inner circle decided to assassinate Makarios through the national guard. Modiano quoted the general as assuring the junta officers, "Don't worry. There will be no consequences if the job is done quickly and neatly."

At a press conference about three weeks later, Kissinger commented on the apparent failure by the U.S. diplomatic and intelligence apparatus to apprehend the coup. "The information was not lying around on the streets," he quipped, observing that Makarios, too, seemed to have been caught by surprise.

Three years later Kissinger was quoted by *Time* (February 28, 1977) in a modest confession of his failure to apprehend the oncoming Cyprus crisis. "If I had ever had twelve hours and been able to pick out an intelligence report," he said, "I would have seen that the situation needed attention."

"I did not expect a coup exactly *that day*," Makarios acknowledged in a private interview. "I was informed by the Greek ambassador that there was to be a meeting in Athens on Monday [July 15]. I thought that after the Monday meeting had been held, I could take whatever precautions were necessary." Makarios had, in fact, been invited by the Greek government to attend the session in Athens, which was described to him as a proceeding to discuss both his letter and the future of Cyprus. "I told the ambassador that I didn't see any reason to go to Athens to discuss those things. I wonder," he mused, a quizzical smile on his face, "what might have happened if I had accepted that kind invitation."

Why did Makarios write his letter?

Chiefly because the Archbishop made the mistake of assuming that his adversaries were rational, he later admitted. "I was under the impression that they would not dare to make a coup immediately," he said. "I thought they could have replied: one, we are not prepared to withdraw the Greek officers or, two, we will withdraw all the Greek officers and break diplomatic relations or, three, make no answer at all." Makarios was also convinced that the junta would not try to topple him at that moment because it would provide the Turks with their long-sought golden opportunity for intervention and the establishment of Turkish military hegemony in Cyprus.

"A coup at this time would not make sense, it would not be reasonable," Makarios insisted one day to a close personal confidant, Cyprus Chief of Public Information Miltiades Cristodoulu. "Of course it would not be reasonable," his aide replied, "but you are not dealing with reasonable people. They are mad."

During an interview in his palace in Cyprus, Makarios described his thinking in moving to a showdown with Athens in this way:

> I have been criticized for showing too much tolerance toward the Greek officers and the Athens presence on the island, for not taking measures before the situation became impossible. It is true that I showed tolerance—but I was hoping to keep the temperature low. Others criticized me because we talked for so many years with the Turks without coming to an agreement. It was suggested that we should come to agreement at least two years ago. Now it is perhaps right to criticize me for this but my critics did not know certain things. . . .
>
> The Greeks were being two-faced. On the diplomatic side, they were stressing independence for Cyprus while on the military side the officers shouted every day for *enosis*. Always the Greek military was trying to undermine intercommunal talks. And so, if we came to an agreement with the Turks on the intercommunal talks, this in the eyes of the Greek military and the EOKA-B organization would have excluded *enosis* with Greece. This is why we talked to the Turks for so many years without coming to an agreement. The fact that we failed to agree probably accounts for the prolongation of my life, politically, and the postponement of the coup.
>
> To those who say why did I write the letter, I point out that even if I did not write the letter, the situation would have deteriorated and the coup would have taken place perhaps two months later. A coup had become almost unavoidable.

By writing the letter, Makarios seized the initiative in his running battle with the junta at a time when there was evidence of serious governmental unraveling in Athens and when the United States was applying formal pressure on the junta to refrain from violence on the island. He may also have been mindful of the two instances in the past decade when the United States acted to prevent the Turks from carrying out de facto partition of the island.

Since the crisis of the mid-1960s, the Archbishop had established quiet understandings with Washington. He agreed tacitly to CIA U-2 flights from the British sovereign base at Akrotiri to overfly the Middle East, to the establishment of radio monitors operated by the CIA's Foreign Broadcast Information Service to eavesdrop on Middle East and Communist bloc traffic, as well as to the establishment of secret antennas that were part of the U.S. electronic-intelligence network. At one point in 1970, the Akrotiri-based U-2s were used to photograph deployment of Soviet missiles along the Suez Canal. In addition, according to one highly placed former intelligence official, the CIA paid Makarios a fixed annual amount—a figure in the $1 million range—into a confidential fund to use for whatever purpose he saw fit. The assumption most widely shared by U.S. diplomatic students of Makarios was that he spent it for pet governmental purposes and did not benefit personally to any substantial degree.

"We were being very good to Makarios in that period," said the former CIA executive. "We were trying to maintain his good will. We warned him when we came upon evidence of an assassination attempt against him [in 1970]." The CIA official conceded, "We were also afraid a botched attempt would take place which would be more trouble than it was worth."

Whatever the private calculus Makarios used in playing his hand, it was a venture with the highest risks to himself and the future of Cyprus. The two great and contradictory currents that had been gathering momentum for more than a generation—the obsession with union coming from the EOKA-B underground and their supporters in the Greek officer corps and the growing Turkish concern over another blood bath in Cyprus—had boiled into a thunderhead that threatened to break imminently over the island. The only realistic hope Makarios might have had at the time was for outside intervention from the United States, the Soviet Union, or both, acting in the spirit of détente. But he was wrong.

If there had ever been a time for strong and imaginative intervention, specifically for stronger U.S. pressure on Athens, it was before the coup and not afterward. Kissinger, by his own account, had not actively involved himself in the worsening spiral of events on Cyprus until after the coup. He may also have concluded that circumstances on the island had not ripened to a point at which intervention would have been productive. In Ankara, the developments were being watched with an awareness of both mounting risk and mounting opportunity. For some ten years, the Turkish army had been rehearsing a combined air and amphibious assault operation that would have been appropriate against only one nearby military target: Cyprus.

On Friday, July 12, Rodger Davies, newly appointed Ambassador to Cyprus, met with Makarios to present his credentials. Davies remarked that he was aware of the reports of coup activity targeted against the Archbishop. "I told him," Makarios ruefully reported months afterward, "that the situation at that time was not dangerous at all—not even serious." In fact, after the session with the new American ambassador, Makarios left for his country palace in the Troodos Mountains to spend the weekend.

The next day, Cyprus intelligence monitored Greek military traffic indicating that there would be a serious development the following Monday. Agents of Makarios intercepted a coded message: "The goods will be loaded at 8 A.M. Monday." A representative of the intelligence service traveled to the Archbishop's weekend retreat to convey the warning. "He laughed again," recalled a close aide to the Archbishop. " 'You are a coward,' he told me as a joke."

On Sunday, July 14, the CIA station in Athens dispatched its message to Washington, suggesting that Ioannides had backed off from his coup intentions. This would be the morning intelligence reading the next day in Washington as the national guard tanks stormed the presidential palace. Several days earlier, British intelligence had also picked up indications that Ioannides was veering away from coup action. But intelligence reports also indicated that the prospect of a backdown by Athens was kindling a violent backlash among the hundreds of Greek officers on Cyprus and in the homeland who were thirsting for the military expedition on Cyprus to achieve *enosis* and liquidate the regime of the red priest. Ioannides was faced with the prospect of an insurrection within the Greek officer cadre in Athens and plotting his downfall in an operation comparable to his own coup against Papadopoulos. Some American intelligence analysts concluded after the coup that Ioannides had also succeeded in duping the CIA in Athens in the July 14 contact. Their assumption is that he had deliberately misinformed his CIA contacts in order to be sure that there would be no last-minute intervention this time by the Americans or British.

What happened after eight o'clock on the morning of July 15 became front-page news that day around the world. Makarios returned from his Troodos retreat and was greeting a delegation of schoolgirls from Egypt. His route back to the palace took him directly past the national guard barracks, which were at the moment on full alert for the coup. As one of the girls in the delegation was addressing him, an aide came in to announce that there was firing against the presidential palace. "Thank you," Makarios said with a smile and then turned back to the Egyptian girl. "Go on with your speech," the Archbishop coaxed. A guard hurried into the room and announced excitedly, "Your Beatitude, there are tanks entering the grounds of the palace." It was at that point that Makarios realized the seriousness of the situation, and he escaped with his bodyguards through the back door of his study, which moments later was demolished by artillery shells. He evaded the guardsmen by dodging through the grounds of the presidential palace, commandeering a car, and escaping to the south.

17. Henry and Aphrodite

Midsummer 1974 was not a particularly suitable time in Washington for yet another international crisis. The country's attention was concentrated on the tragic spectacle of the collapse of presidential government in the Watergate crisis. Congress was moving toward impeachment of the President and federal juries were hearing evidence that would bring criminal verdicts against some of the President's highest-ranking subordinates. Secretary of State Kissinger found himself enmeshed as well in the toils of the scandal. His denials that he had ordered the wiretapping of government officials and journalists seemed to be contradicted by evidence coming out of the House Judiciary Committee's files, and the secretary's probity was being openly questioned. Kissinger had issued his angry denial to these charges at Salzburg and threatened to resign unless Congress, specifically the Senate Foreign Relations Committee, cleared his name. In addition, the various pots of international crisis were at full boil.

In the Middle East, the secretary was trying to avert the outbreak of another war, which some in Washington were already pronouncing inevitable. In Moscow, Kissinger was pursuing delicate strategic arms negotiations from a sharply divided base of domestic opinion on how far the United States should go. The administration's trade policy with the Soviet Union was also under heavy domestic attack, with Kissin-

ger's critics, notably Senator Henry Jackson (D-Washington), holding
the trade bill hostage to the issue of Moscow's treatment of Jews and
dissident intellectuals. From the lofty heights of the seventh floor of
the State Department, Cyprus was a far-off blip on Henry Kissinger's
storm charts.

And so when the first news of the coup in Cyprus reached Washington shortly after midnight, there was an initial spasm of indecision
and confusion. The first reports of the death of Makarios did not
produce undiluted sorrow in Foggy Bottom. One official, on learning
by Monday morning, Washington time, that the Archbishop had survived, remarked in a telephone conversation with a Greek diplomat,
"How inconvenient."

At 12:30 P.M. on the day of the coup, the American Secretary of
State received Cyprus's ambassador, Nikos Dimitriu, and engaged him
in perfunctory banter, which the Cypriot diplomat found unseemly in
the face of his national crisis. Who is Nikos Sampson? Kissinger
asked Dimitriu. The ambassador replied by reciting the reputation of
the newly installed President of Cyprus as a "paranoid" and an "egomaniac."

"But I have been called an egomaniac, too," Kissinger responded
with a smile.

"You should not compare yourself with Sampson, Mr. Secretary,"
Dimitriu answered grimly.

At that point, the American Secretary of State stated what he
wished to be considered his provisional policy under the confused
circumstances of the moment. Normally, he explained to the visiting
Cypriot delegation, it was the policy of the State Department in the
event of a coup to recognize the de facto government. "This we will
not do," he said. "We will wait and see. I have not yet gotten a full
report from the Embassy." The fact that he agreed to see Dimitriu,
Kissinger explained, signified that he still recognized the legitimacy
of the ousted government in Nicosia.

Some of the onlookers were struck by the absence in Kissinger's
remarks of even perfunctory words of condolence to the representatives of the ousted government. "He didn't seem to attach much seriousness to what had happened," one participant recalled.

Throughout the first week of the crisis, the day-to-day voice of
American foreign policy was that of Ambassador Robert Anderson,
the State Department's press spokesman at the daily noon briefings.

Anderson was an amiable and long-suffering bureaucrat whose job, despite the most persistent heckling of press inquisitors, was to reflect faithfully in word and nuance what Kissinger wanted said—and not to stray an inch from the secretary's guidelines.

To anyone familiar with the secret diplomatic history prior to the onset of the coup, Anderson's statements were confused and disingenuous. They presented a picture of a vacillating American policy toward both Makarios and the regime that had violently displaced him. On the day of the coup, Anderson faced a crowded room of newsmen and confined himself to the bland declaration that "our policy remains that of supporting the independence and territorial integrity of Cyprus and its constitutional arrangements and we urge all other states to support a similar policy." In the next breath, Anderson responded that the United States had been engaged in no "negotiations, secret talks, cable traffic" to avert the coup. Most significant was what the United States did *not* say that day. While the action of Athens was being decried throughout Europe, Secretary Kissinger's spokesman did not utter a word of criticism of the intervention from Greece, not a word to deplore the reported assassination of Makarios.

Despite the thousands of words of cable traffic between the State Department and the embassies in Athens and Nicosia over the previous months on the dangers of an Athens-launched coup, Anderson said at a later briefing when asked if there had been outside intervention in the Cyprus crisis, "No. In our view, there has been no outside intervention." Addressing himself to the same point in a later conversation, a prominent Cypriot politician said: "It was as though a foreign power had taken over control of the United States and installed Al Capone in the White House."

For the first three days after the coup, Anderson defensively parried questions bearing on U.S. recognition of the Sampson regime. "The present situation on Cyprus is unclear," he said on Tuesday, July 16. "And in our view, as of the moment, the question of recognition does not arise."

"Is the Makarios government the government of Cyprus at the moment as far as we're concerned?" a reporter asked.

"I would rather just not comment on it at all."

On the seventeenth: "Bob, which government do we recognize as of now?"

"I just said over here now that, as of this time, we are trying to evaluate the situation and there is no question of . . . we are trying to decide, let me put it that way."

On the eighteenth, Anderson was asked about the lead story in the *New York Times* that morning, which said, ". . . high American officials indicated that the Nixon Administration was leaning more toward Nikos Sampson . . . than toward Archbishop Makarios."

Anderson said, "I think that as far as our current policy, I am going to refer you to what I have been saying for the last two or three days here on Cyprus. I am not going to take it any further. . . ."

He was then asked, "Was the secretary meeting with Makarios on Monday, July 22, as a private citizen, as Archbishop, or as President of Cyprus?"

Anderson answered, "He's meeting with *Archbishop* Makarios on Monday."

The tenor of official American response to the crisis appeared, at least, to be tilting toward the puppet regime in Nicosia installed by Athens. In Great Britain, by contrast, as in other countries of Europe and in Moscow, there were unstinting declarations of public support for the ousted Cypriot leader.

Kissinger afterward explained in private audiences with newsmen the rationale for the State Department's seemingly passive role. "Emotional" (Kissinger's word) underlings in the department wanted him to make strong declarations against Athens and Sampson. He, on the other hand, felt that any public proclamations against the Cypriot puppet president would be used by the Turks to justify intervention. The secretary's feeling was that he did not want the Turks to be able to use the statements of Anderson or any other U.S. spokesman as their invitation card to invasion.

Kissinger reached the quick conclusion, according to well-documented background accounts afterward, that the Turks this time, unlike 1964 and 1967, could not be deterred from invading. And yet, in the meetings of the President's crisis-reaction team headed by Kissinger, the Washington Special Action Group (WASAG), the prevailing policy line from the day of the coup onward was that the United States depended on its air and naval bases in Greece and would do nothing to jeopardize them with the present or any future government. Furthermore, Kissinger was apprehensive that the downfall of the Ioannides government might be followed by a new clique of younger officers with an anti-U.S., anti-Western position.

During the secret WASAG deliberations, there was a fear expressed of a revolution, similar to the one led by Colonel Muammar el-Qaddafi in Libya. Since Kissinger felt the United States did not want to take the responsibility for what happened next in Greece, he was reluctant to use the full force of American leverage to influence the events. Washington was not betting on the restoration of constitutional government in Greece; there was little indication of such a possibility in the intelligence readings, although Secretary Kissinger was all too glad to share in the credit when it came to a political happy ending in the form of the recall by the military of exiled leader Constantine Karamanlis.

Kissinger's own diplomacy after the Greek coup was conducted by telephone through one-on-one personal contacts. There were many calls to Turkish Prime Minister Bulent Ecevit, his former seminar student, as well as to other players in the melodrama. Little was written down on paper or passed on to others who were also trying at the working level to grapple with the crisis. The bureaucracy was, as it always was under Kissinger, in the dark. Distrustful of his desk officers, whom he regarded as agents for their country clients, supremely confident in his own conception of events, Kissinger plied the telephone circuits to Ankara, Athens, and London, while the East Mediterranean specialists of the State Department were reaching a point of near revolt because of the confused and careening direction of American policy at the top.

The main problem with Kissinger's high-wire diplomacy was that there were no witnesses and no recorded minutes of what was being done at the center of the diplomatic process. Contradictions between private background accounts and the public evidence quickly became apparent. For example, Kissinger told reporters during an in-flight backgrounder that he had privately assured Ecevit prior to the Turkish invasion that Sampson was unacceptable to the United States. And yet, when the *New York Times* reported prominently on the third day of the coup that the administration was leaning toward recognition of Sampson, the assertion went virtually unchallenged by the State Department. This could not have escaped official attention in Ankara. At the Ministry of Foreign Affairs in Ankara, a Turkish senior diplomat maintained during an interview several months after the event that he and his colleagues were convinced during the first few days of the crisis that the United States was on the verge of recognizing the

Sampson regime. "We felt that if we delayed our intervention," he said, "America was going to recognize Sampson. We read the statements by Robert Anderson. I told my government that the United States would recognize Sampson if you don't move now."

From this contradictory record of testimony, one conclusion emerges clearly about Kissinger's intention in the aftermath of the violent overthrow of the Makarios government. It was, unlike the Johnson administration in the mid-1960s crisis, to do as little as possible: not to antagonize the Greek junta, which sponsored the coup, not to decry the regime of the Cypriot assassin Sampson, not to invoke against Turkey the political sanctions against invasion that the Johnson administration had been willing to employ.

At the State Department, the policy differences between the seventh floor and the working-level specialists on the fourth floor were further exacerbated by the next installment of the crisis, the onset of the Turkish invasion. Kissinger's attitude toward the lower tier of the bureaucracy, which he suspected of leaking unflattering references to his strategies, were most vividly expressed in a session with newsmen aboard *Air Force One*. When one questioner started to cite reports that he was somehow implicated in the downfall of Makarios, Kissinger snapped, "Oh, cut that out. For God's sake. . . . One of my pet phobias with the press is you guys are all running around all day picking up sixth-hand crap from eighth-level officials!"

18. The Sisco Intervention and the Invasion

On the night of July 17, Kissinger dispatched Undersecretary of State for Political Affairs Joseph Sisco to the East Mediterranean on what the experts, including Sisco himself, knew to be a Mission Impossible —to prevent the Turks from invading. Sisco was not new to such negotiations. He had accompanied George Ball ten years earlier on a parallel mission to stop the Turks from landing on Cyprus and initiating a full-scale Mediterranean war. In Ball's case, there had been more favorable odds for a settlement. A constitutional government had ruled in Athens, unlike the outcast Ioannides regime. More important, Ball had the powerful diplomatic deterrent of the letter Lyndon Johnson had written to the Turks. The humiliation of the Johnson letter and the 1967 intervention by the United States were still rankling in the Turkish national memory when Sisco embarked on his mission with a virtually empty attaché case, a smile, and a shoeshine.

The Turks were now in no mood for compromise. Ankara had just told the United States it was going to abrogate restrictions on opium production, an action that brought U.S. Ambassador to Turkey William Macomber back to Washington for consultation at the time of the coup in Cyprus. The descendants of the Ottoman Empire were no longer of a mood to tolerate abuses by their former subjects—the Greek Cypriots. The golden opportunity had finally come. In the words of a Turkish diplomat who was deeply involved in the Washington end of the crisis, "The Greeks committed the unbelievably stupid move of appointing Sampson, giving us the opportunity to solve our problems once and for all. Unlike 1964 and 1967, the United States leverage on us in 1974 was minimal. We could no longer be scared off by threats of the Soviet bogeyman."

July 18. All paths now converged on London. It was Sisco's first stop for consultation with British Foreign Minister James Callaghan, who was to play the role of front man in the later diplomatic efforts at Geneva to settle the Cyprus conflict. It was also an obligatory stop-over point for Ecevit, who was required under the terms of the 1960 London-Zurich agreement to consult with Turkey's co-guarantor power, Great Britain, before taking the ultimate step of military intervention. Kissinger was on the telephone, from time to time, with each of the three principals.

In an evening meeting at 10 Downing Street, the Turkish Prime Minister set out his country's objectives. He asked the British, first of all, to join with Turkey in joint military action against the Greek junta's forces in Cyprus. Prime Minister Harold Wilson and Callaghan said no. They argued that such an involvement would destroy London's usefulness as a good broker in reaching an eventual solution. Also, there were 10,000 British dependents on the island and 30,000 British tourists in Greece, all of whom were potential hostages. Furthermore, there were 9,000 British troops on Cyprus, only a small part of which could perform a combat role, the major portion being needed to police the two sovereign bases at Akrotiri and Dhekelia along with the extensive radio and radar networks that dot many mountaintops on the Cypriot landscape. Also the sovereign bases themselves were of crucial military and intelligence concern to the British. Would the British then make the bases available as staging areas for the Turkish forces? Regretfully, no, the British replied.

Upon his arrival, Sisco sat down to a long luncheon session with Ecevit and heard the terms for deferring the invasion course upon which it was becoming increasingly clear that Turkey was determined to embark. The 650 Greek officers had to be withdrawn, as Makarios had himself already asked. Sampson had to be squelched. Furthermore, there would have to be agreement on the establishment of a federal state with Turkish and Greek components, permanent access to the sea for Turkish forces from Kyrenia, restoration of Makarios (an early position later rescinded), and stringent U.N. measures to prevent illegal traffic of arms into Cyprus. In short, it was a list of demands that had little prospect of being achieved in Athens. Nonetheless, Ecevit agreed to allow time for Sisco to test the atmosphere for concessions in Athens. Perhaps thirty-six hours. It was already well into the evening.

Sisco, who had arrived with a smile, emerged with a grim face from the room where he had conferred with Ecevit for some seven hours. Ecevit had told him that the Turkish army was on alert. Unless the Greeks were willing to meet the terms, Turkey would have to carry out its responsibilities as a guarantor. Sisco promised to bring back a response from Athens by sundown the next day. The American envoy and the Turkish Prime Minister met again at Heathrow Airport, where their planes were waiting. Sisco's final words to Ecevit in London were, "Don't do anything until we consult again."

Before his departure, Sisco had wired Washington that his mood was pessimistic. The Turks were strong in their views. The only hope was to start a diplomatic dialogue of some sort between Greece and Turkey. "We are on the brink of hostilities," Sisco wired home. He also confessed that he wasn't sure that Ecevit was not merely going through the motions of consultation to prepare the legal grounds for military intervention.

Ecevit, upon arriving in Ankara, went directly to a meeting of the Turkish cabinet and military commanders. He informed them that he was awaiting a reply from Sisco the next evening. The generals were impatient. They wanted to begin the countdown for the invasion, and they needed time to reach the shores of Cyprus.

July 19. His exasperation with the Greeks and the American embassy growing, Sisco was unable to make contact immediately with what passed for governing authority in Athens. Finally, on Friday afternoon, with time running out, Sisco was able to arrange a meeting with Ioannides, Armed Forces Chief of Staff General Gregorios Bonanos, and Prime Minister Androutsopoulos. Sisco told the Greeks of his conversation with Ecevit and the intolerability to the Turks of the Sampson regime in Nicosia. He asked what steps the Greeks were prepared to take that might lead to a resumption of talks between the two governments. To moderate his grim message to the Greeks,

Sisco assured them that "I come here as a friend and a representative of a NATO ally."

Ioannides excused himself after some twenty minutes, remarking only that "Greece is Greece." The others agreed grudgingly to replace rather than withdraw the Greek officers on Cyprus on a phased timetable. Sisco had no leverage to apply, and he knew that he had not obtained the price of settlement, if it were achievable at all, in Athens that night.

He flew off to Ankara and was by nine o'clock that night closeted with U.S. Ambassador William Macomber in the American embassy. Sisco, recounted one of the senior members of the American diplomatic team in Ankara, "had goddamn little to bring. He had nothing, in fact. We knew it wasn't enough."

For days, the Turkish press had been exhorting Ecevit to go to Cyprus. There was a drumbeat of public criticism at the delay in making the move whose time had never seemed so opportune. Leftist student demonstrators were carrying signs through the streets of Ankara that said of the Sisco mission: "Sisco-Fiasco." "Everyone was asking," a U.S. official recalled, "what the hell was Ecevit waiting for? The opportunity was there. Sampson was more famous in Turkey than he had been in Britain during the EOKA insurrection. He was a killer of Turkish civilians."

When Macomber and Sisco sat down finally with Ecevit, it was about midnight on the nineteenth. The Turkish National Security Council had met and given the green light to the invasion. The cabinet was now meeting, the last chance to forestall invasion.

Sisco tried to put as positive a light as he could on the fruitless talks in Athens. Ecevit listened thoughtfully. Sisco at one point remarked to Ecevit, who was an accomplished poet and translator of English verse, "You have given all your life to humanitarianism, to the spirit of liberty. Now as a result of your decision a lot of people are going to be dead. Why can't you wait forty-eight hours?"

Suddenly the Turkish Prime Minister became icy. Ecevit said that the Turks did not want to repeat the mistakes of history, of 1964 and 1967. "The United States and Turkey both have made mistakes—the United States by preventing Turkish military action and Turkey by accepting. We should not make the same mistakes again."

Sisco and Macomber retired to the embassy to await the verdict of the cabinet. Sisco cabled Kissinger of his deepening pessimism. The

American diplomats sat in Macomber's upstairs sitting room, trying to figure out what to say next. At about 4:00 A.M., Ecevit again received Sisco and the American ambassador and informed them of the collective decision. "We have done it your way for ten years," Ecevit proclaimed, "and now we are going to do it our way." To Sisco's plea for forty-eight more hours, the Turkish Prime Minister said, "You now have—848 hours."

July 20. At dawn, Sisco stood alone on the tarmac of the airport in Ankara, awaiting a plane back to Athens. A Turkish armada was steaming toward the northern coast of Cyprus. Deeply depressed by his humiliating ordeal in both capitals, Sisco contacted Washington and suggested that he return home. Kissinger's response, recalled by a member of the Washington task force who inadvertently intercepted the traffic, was to threaten that he would go to the East Mediterranean himself to take over the crisis mediation. It was not clear whether the secretary was joking or not.

Sisco plodded back to Athens, embarked now on the task of helping to arrange a cease-fire. At this point, the forces of political disintegration in Athens were working in favor of the American diplomat rather than against him. For the next two days and nights, Sisco and the American embassy staff sought to assemble enough of the Greek government to arrange for a cease-fire.

On the morning of the twentieth, Sisco went into a meeting at the Greek Pentagon with Tasca and the commander of Hellenic forces, General Bonanos. "We tried to stop the Greeks from escalating with our assurances that we could stop the Turks from going any further," said one of the American participants in the session. The Americans, of course, had no basis at this point for any such assurances. At noon, Sisco went into a session with the new Greek Foreign Minister Constantine Kypraios as the Greek general staff was calling a general mobilization for war. Greek troops were already massed in the northern region of Thrace as a result of prior tensions over the Aegean oil issue.

Secretly, Ioannides and his closest advisers were preparing orders for submarine and aerial attacks on the invading Turkish forces, whose first amphibious landing was being hampered by adverse weather. However, unbeknown to Ioannides, a mutiny was beginning to form among his top military commanders who were against full-scale war with Turkey. There were strong indications afterward that the American intelligence establishment in Athens was now monitoring the generals' revolt against Ioannides. Afterward, in fact, the deposed head of the junta was to charge through his attorneys that the generals conspired with the Americans in what the attorneys regarded as a treasonous scheme to betray his orders. It was also alleged that the Americans had passed on assurances through the CIA that the Turks would not invade if the coup on Cyprus were cleanly executed and the rights of the Turkish minority were assured.

The fighting in Cyprus on the twentieth reflected, appropriately enough, the confusions of the entire crisis. The following account was given by a Greek cabinet-level official who had access to the classified records of the battle that day.

> Even as the Turkish ships were steaming toward the shore, the Greeks had no orders from their commanders to shoot. The national guard was sending messages: "The ships are coming, there are planes overhead. But we have no orders to fire." It was only when the Turkish paratroopers began landing over Nicosia that a reaction was ordered by the Greek commanders.
>
> On the ground were less than 500 Greek officers. The national guard was not at full strength. It had been weakened by internal fighting and defections. Many of the mobilized guardsmen took their guns and went home. The brunt of the fighting on the Greek side was done by 4,500 Cypriots and 400 Greek officers. Tell me how can you fight an air force and marines without air support? The Greeks, I must say, fought like lions. Even though they may have been pro-junta and the assassins of Makarios, I have to admit they fought bravely without air or artillery support, taking heavy casualties. Yet, they lasted forty-eight hours under heavy air and naval bombardment. Their casualties were 50 percent dead or wounded.

That night, the Greeks flew in a company of some 300 commandos in fifteen aircraft, landing under Turkish fire. Here, again, the casualties were ferocious.

Sisco flew back to Ankara in the evening despite warnings from the Turks that they could not guarantee air safety. At one point in the trip, he wondered aloud in which direction he was headed.

July 21. On Sunday morning, the heads of the Hellenic armed services assembled in the Greek Pentagon, a five-minute taxi ride from the American embassy where Sisco, Tasca, and the embassy staff were trying to find a quorum of governmental authority in Athens. Finally, an aide-de-camp to Ioannides, a Colonel Loukoutos, entered the office of General Bonanos.

"Gentlemen," said Loukoutos, "a decision has been taken to attack Turkey on all fronts: Cyprus, Thrace, everywhere. Prepare yourselves, gentlemen; the decision has been made."

Army Chief of Staff Andreas Galatsanos was the first to respond. "I am not ready to enter an aggressive war," he said. "I'm ready for defense but not aggression." Others began to voice reservations about the decision being imposed upon them by Ioannides.

Air Force Chief of Staff Alexander Papanikolaou was the next to speak. "The air force is ready to carry out its duty, but an air attack would be unwise and have no decisive results," he told Loukoutos. Ioannides had wanted six Phantoms based in Crete to provide air support for the beleaguered Greek officers and the remaining force of national guardsmen who had not defected from the junta. Loukoutos stared around the room at the assembled chiefs and then left curtly to report to his chief. The generals remained locked in an all-day discussion of what to do next.

Sisco returned in the late morning from Ankara, where he had been trying to carry on the cease-fire discussions. He spent most of the day vainly trying to make contact with the evaporating government of Greece. Prime Minister Androutsopoulos, by the account of Greek and American sources, was at this stage of the crisis suffering a nervous breakdown—trembling and incoherent.

While the cease-fire efforts were in progress, the Turks began charging that a Greek armada was heading for Cyprus, disguised under the Turkish flag. American military aides were told by Greek counterparts in the Athens Pentagon, "If the Turks think they are our ships, let them sink them." Meanwhile, at the Pentagon in Washington, a computer run was hastily conducted to ascertain the location of every American vessel in the theater. A confusing factor was that all the ships in the vicinity were of American make and supplied under military aid programs to both NATO allies. The confusion over the alleged Greek ships reached a point of high comedy. At Kissinger's home in Washington, the telephone rang early in the morning, according to an authoritative source. It was Ecevit on the line, complaining of the Greek armada moving toward the embattled island. "Those perfidious Greeks, you know what they are now doing? They are flying Turkish flags to try to fool our aircraft." Nancy Kissinger grumbled sleepily to her husband, "Why don't you tell him to shut up and sink the goddamn things?" As it happened, the Turks did just that but then discovered, too late, that their aerial reconnaissance was in error. The toll was one Turkish ship sunk and two damaged.

By midnight, Sisco was in the office of General Bonanos with the Greek Chief of Naval Operations, Admiral Petros Arapakis, at his side. The American emissary spoke on the phone with Kissinger, who had just been on the phone with Ecevit. The secretary explained that Ecevit had agreed to a cease-fire at 2:00 P.M. the next day but had to convene a meeting of the Turkish National Security Council to ratify the decision. Sisco hung up and explained the situation to Bonanos, insisting that the Greeks make an announcement of the impending cease-fire as soon as Kissinger called back with the final confirmation from Ecevit. Bonanos said he and his associates wanted to sleep on it, since the cease-fire would not take effect until 2:00 P.M. the next day. He left.

July 22. At 2:00 A.M., Kissinger phoned Sisco back to report that the Turks were in full accord on the cessation of hostilities in Cyprus. Now the Greeks must agree. At this point, Sisco realized with mounting dread and frustration that the Greek government was nowhere to be found. "This is the goddamnedest government I have ever had to deal with," Sisco raged as he tried through the American embassy staff to reach some Greek principals. The Prime Minister was not at home. Bonanos couldn't be found. Ioannides, as always, was nowhere to be found. Finally, at 2:40 A.M., Sisco and Tasca tracked down Admiral Arapakis, who was asleep in his office.

Would the Greek government accept a cease-fire, Sisco desperately asked the naval Chief of Staff. "Yes," the admiral answered. Sisco persisted, "But can you speak for your government?" Arapakis asked for time to determine that.

The admiral rang through immediately to Androutsopoulos and Bonanos, who had not been at home to Sisco. "The Americans are fooling us," Androutsopoulos said. "Wait until tomorrow, and we will try to make a decision." Bonanos also equivocated. So did Foreign Minister Kypraios. Finally, Arapakis called Sisco back and said, yes, he had the sanction of his government. "Did you get the concurrence of General Ioannides?" he was asked. "Yes," Arapakis lied.

With this gambit, the Greek admiral, the most audacious of the conspirators, set the stage for the final act in the downfall of Ioannides and seven years of military dictatorship in Greece. The cease-fire was proclaimed for 2:00 P.M.

Later in the morning, the chiefs of the Hellenic armed services assembled in the plush, paneled suite in the general staff building, which former military ruler George Papadopoulos had refurbished at a cost of $230,000. In line with their previous day's discussion, they notified President Ghizikis that things could not go on under Ioannides and that the civilian politicians would have to be called back to power. Ghizikis agreed. The decision was communicated to Ioannides, who promptly joined the commanders. They were wrong, Ioannides stonily told the joint chiefs. He had issued orders. Greece was ready to go to war.

Icily, Air Force Chief of Staff Papanikolaou recalled Ioannides's position as the mere Chief of Military Police, a rank lower than that of anyone in the room. "In the name of my country and my children," Papanikolaou said, "I don't accept here a decision on such an important matter by a subordinate of ours. We must not accept it." It was the first time since Ioannides had seized power in November that anyone had dared to pull formal rank on him.

Ioannides got up and slapped the table. "It seems that General Papanikolaou doesn't know me," the junta leader spat out. The Air Force Chief of Staff answered, "And it is clear that you don't know *me*. If you think you can act now, then remember, General, that I have the means to stop you."

Ghizikis interrupted. "Gentlemen, the country is in danger. We must not quarrel," he ordered. Ioannides realized that power had finally slipped from his hands and he acceded to demands by his former collaborators that he not oppose their decision to call back the civilians.

"We have been betrayed," he later stormed to a few remaining loyal subordinates. "We have been betrayed in Cyprus and now here in Athens." His surrender was only tactical, he assured them. They would lie in wait for an opportunity to reassume power in the shambles of governmental transition.

By 1:00 P.M., invitations were going to the homes of the civilian leaders who had survived the seven years of junta rule for a meeting in the office of Ghizikis the following day. Sisco finally left for home. The danger of war had now subsided.

19. Tilt to Turkey

On July 23, there was a gathering in Athens such as the capital had not seen since the heavy curtain of dictatorship had descended on April 21, 1967. Gathered around the table with the generals, the usurpers of Greek democracy, were three former civilian premiers: Panayiotis Kanellopoulos, seventy-two-year-old leader of the National Radical Union party; George Atanasiades-Novas; and Spyros Markezines. Also present were Center Union party leader George Mavros, former Foreign Minister Evangelos Averof-Tositsas, former Defense Minister Petros Garoufalias, and Xenophon Zolotas, former governor of the Bank of Greece.

The military leaders said they wanted a government installed as soon as possible. The civilians took the joint stand that any government that was to be formed needed a wide base of popular support. After two hours of discussion, a consensus emerged that there were only two figures of sufficient national stature to lead the new Greek government out of the chaos of the moment—Kanellopoulos and exiled former President Constantine Karamanlis.

Averof, an agile political operator and a man with strong Western allegiances and conservative leanings, openly endorsed Karamanlis. Meanwhile, Kanellopoulos and Mavros agreed to privately discuss their prospects for establishing a broad coalition government, which everyone agreed the former would need in order to rule effectively.

"Only Karamanlis can handle this," Averof persisted with Ghizikis.

"The coalition [is] not the solution. The situation is too explosive." Ghizikis protested that Karamanlis was in Paris, that it would take too much time. Averof took out his address book. "He could be here in three hours. Let me call him."

There was no answer at the residence. While the military men grew increasingly impatient, Averof reached a cousin of Karamanlis's who reacted at first with incredulity and then agreed to take a taxi and give Karamanlis the telephone number of General Ghizikis.

"I need twenty-four hours," Karamanlis initially responded when Averof asked him to come immediately to Athens to reassume the job he had quit eleven years earlier in a dispute with the royal family. The generals, one by one, spoke to the former Prime Minister. He agreed finally to fly from Paris immediately. The news flew quickly out of the room.

By midday, cheering crowds and honking automobile horns were evidence of the euphoria that swept Athens at the demise of the junta and the return of democracy to its place of birth. A cease-fire was in effect in Cyprus, and Greece was on the road back to constitutional government.

At 11:00 P.M., Ambassador Tasca received a call from Mavros, asking him to come to the office of outgoing President Ghizikis and "share our joy." The ambassador accepted and joined the extraordinary transitional celebration that was awaiting the return of Karamanlis. Tasca put in a call to Kissinger, who spoke to Mavros and Kanellopoulos. "The secretary told us, 'That's swell,' " an American participant remembered. "The Greeks were showing us fantastic cordiality. They wanted us to be with them at this very important moment."

In Cyprus, meanwhile, Sampson abdicated, disappearing as quickly as he had arisen on command from Athens. His replacement was Glafkos Clerides, the Speaker of the House and successor, under the 1960 constitution, to the President. Clerides, a lawyer and former Royal Air Force pilot who had won his political spurs in the EOKA movement, was well respected in Cyprus and by far the favorite with the Americans over the stubborn and politically mercurial Archbishop Makarios, whom the majority of Greek Cypriots regarded as their true national leader.

It would seem that a moment had arrived, a state of equilibrium among the contending interests, that the diplomatic managers might have tried to freeze into the status quo. Turkey had established by military arms its long-sought "access to the sea"; Greece and Cyprus were rid of their respective dictatorships. The new civilian government of Karamanlis could be expected to pursue a line of constructive support for the intercommunal talks in Cyprus that had come earlier in the year to a closer point of conciliation than ever in their six-year history. Even if Makarios were to return, he would no longer feel the hot breath of the junta-backed EOKA-B movement on his neck. Hostilities were ended, or so it seemed several days later when the three sides went to Geneva and ratified the cease-fire on July 30.

In Washington, there was a sense of relief at having muddled through another East Mediterranean crisis with Kissinger's telephonic choreography ("rolling negotiations, a drafting exercise by transatlantic telephone," one State Department official called it) and more than a little bit of luck. The irony of the finale in Athens was that the same Greek military leadership that supinely acquiesced and then collaborated with the junta had now returned the government to the civilians.

And so, once again in Washington, a major turning point was reached, a new crossroads for American policy.

On the one hand, there was the continuing course of official passivity in Washington, with occasional public words of exhortation for moderation, peace, and reasonableness. On the other hand was the perception of the extent of Turkish determination to exploit the opportunity of the moment. Turkey now faced across the Aegean a fragile democratic order in Athens with a military force that had been purged of the cream of its leadership and ravaged by the incompetent rule of the colonels. Washington opted for words; Turkey, for action. On the day of the cease-fire, July 22, Ecevit declared in a press conference that "Turkish presence on the island is now irrevocably established." The ten-mile corridor from Kyrenia to the Turkish sector of Nicosia, he said, "will be a permanent base of strength for the Turkish people on the island." The introspective poet had achieved a military victory in Cyprus that brought him to the highest point of popularity of any Turkish leader since Kemal Ataturk. He would not surrender the initiative lightly.

From the beginning of the cease-fire agreement, the Turkish forces steadily nibbled their way out of the Kyrenia corridor in a low-level prolongation of the war.

Representatives of Greece, Turkey, and Great Britain sat down for their first round of talks at Geneva from July 25 to July 30. The first stage of the talks was intended to achieve three urgent objectives: stopping the hostilities, stabilizing the situation on the ground, and laying the groundwork for final negotiations on a permanent peaceful solution of the Cyprus problem that would preserve the island's independence and territorial integrity.

But there was only partial compliance by both sides with the first objective. The Turkish occupation forces kept inching forward amid reports of pillage and violence directed at Greek-Cypriot villagers. But also the Greek-Cypriot forces, which were required to withdraw from Turkish enclaves they had occupied after the invasion, provided only lagging compliance with the Geneva provision. The most blatant transgressions of the July 22 cease-fire were committed, however, by the Turkish army, with its mastery of the air over the island and its modern American equipment, which included heavy tanks, mobile artillery, and armored personnel carriers. The Greek national guard had only limited equipment and no air force. Turkish military advances during the first Geneva talks almost collapsed the negotiations. Clerides at one point threatened, "It will be with the greatest reluctance that I will appear before the Greek-Cypriot people and invite them to fight to the last man to the end. But the Turkish advances are forcing me to take a step I am loath to make."

Washington paid scant attention to the flouting of the July 30 cease-fire agreement. Anderson replied to press questions on the violations with his famous equivocations. Asked on August 2 about the Turkish cease-fire violations on Cyprus, Anderson responded, "We hope that as the secretary has said many times now, that the United Nations can take as active a role as possible in trying to restore peace and stability on the island to make the cease-fire as effective as possible."

He was asked, "Has the secretary been on the phone again—to the Turkish prime minister or the Turkish officials in Ankara?"

Anderson replied: "I have no knowledge that he has recently been on the phone to either the prime minister or the Turkish officials."

On a mistaken note of high optimism, the second Geneva conference was convened on August 8 with British Foreign Secretary Callaghan in the chair and all five parties to the dispute represented: the three guarantor powers—Britain, Greece, and Turkey—as well as the Greek-Cypriot and Turkish-Cypriot representatives, Clerides and Rauf Denktash.

Despite the growing Greek outrage at the Turkish military advances under the cover of the cease-fire, Kissinger was confident that all the outstanding differences between the two sides would be settled in Geneva. In his mind, the military crisis was settled with the cease-fire and Geneva I, and the political and diplomatic issues would be resolved at Geneva II. The British, also, were confident of a solution during the second Geneva discussions—so much so that Callaghan moved ahead the schedule of the conference from August 21 to August 8 and declined Kissinger's offer of a senior American representative. "Callaghan foresaw a great diplomatic triumph and a domestic victory," said one high-ranking American official. Kissinger, who had announced the earlier cease-fire in Washington not too subtly underscoring the role of his own diplomacy, was also hoping for yet another triumph.

What Washington and London failed to recognize was that Turkey had come to Geneva in no mood to compromise its gains and, in fact, determined to impose its final solution to the Cyprus crisis in accordance with the "new realities" on the island. That solution was called federation and meant a de facto partition. Weak as the Greek position was as it emerged from the recent government crisis, neither Athens nor the Greek-Cypriot leadership was prepared to accept these terms.

Geneva was "a totally screwed-up situation," as Kissinger himself was to describe it, under Callaghan's chairmanship. Callaghan had seriously overestimated the prospects for settlement, and the Americans had mistakenly accepted the British diagnosis, as Kissinger later saw it. The British were aware of Washington's lack of appreciation for their role. And in Whitehall, a Foreign Office official deeply involved in the Cyprus question responded, "From the beginning we approached the situation with the attitude that Henry is going to do it. We did not repudiate our responsibility but we needed support from the United States." That support meant pressure on Turkey, which the United States as chief arms supplier was uniquely equipped to apply.

At the second Geneva convention, the fundamental issues were these: Turkey, by virtue of its military power position in the island, wanted to scrap the framework of the 1960 London-Zurich agreement establishing the Republic of Cyprus as a sovereign republic with a single government structure embodying the two communities. The Greeks and Greek Cypriots wanted to preserve the republic in its basic 1960 framework, although they were now willing to adopt constitutional revisions designed to safeguard the rights of the Turkish minority. The United States, which had no constitutional standing as a member of the conference, was a powerful outside broker who didn't care how a settlement was reached so long as the threatened breach in the southern wall of the NATO military alliance was patched. Great Britain was the referee, trying to maintain order and keep the diplomatic ball in play while Kissinger tried to bring his leverage to bear behind the scenes. The Soviet Union also maintained a presence in the wings at Geneva to monitor the proceedings and advance its chief interest: maintaining a sovereign, integral, and nonaligned Cyprus free of NATO entanglements through extension of Greek or Turkish hegemony on the island.

If the United States wished at that point to press for a solution that included the preservation of the Cyprus republic on its 1960 constitutional foundations, it had only one course at Geneva. That was to press the Turks to accept their expanded position won by force of arms and to restart the machinery of intercommunal negotiation between the Greek-Cypriot and Turkish-Cypriot factions. A way had to be found toward a more workable system—providing more security for the Turkish minority—than did the 1960 London-Zurich agreement.

But the evidence suggests that for Kissinger, the issue of the constitutional integrity of the Republic of Cyprus was a mote of legal abstraction that had little to do with solving the problems at hand. The Turks, meanwhile, took the position that all constitutional bets were off and the London-Zurich commitments abrogated in 1963 by Makarios when he scrapped the Turkish veto written into the original agreement.

Turkey at this point was the master of the ground. It was also, in Washington's eyes, far more important now as a military ally. It had a standing army of half a million. It lay astride the southern border of the Soviet Union, and it also contained some two dozen installations including a number of powerful electronic monitoring stations that provided military intelligence from within the Soviet Union. Turkey was also the most forward base for the stationing of U.S. and NATO nuclear weapons. Greece, on the other hand, was now ruled by a civilian government with an uncertain political future. Its army was less than half the size of Turkey's, and its military leadership was decimated by the seven years of junta rule and the most recent trauma of government change.

Prior to Geneva II, the American silence in the face of the day-by-day record of Turkish cease-fire violations signaled the swing of the pendulum of opinion in Washington toward Ankara. Once Geneva began, Kissinger took the initiative in trying to help the Turks achieve their objective of writing a new political future for Cyprus in a manner that at the time would allow the new Greek government to save face. According to Haluk Ulman, Ecevit's Foreign Adviser, Kissinger told the Turks that "it would be difficult for both the Greek government and the Cypriot Greek leaders to accept a federation based on two separate regions, for it would appear as a division of the island into two, placing one part under Turkish hegemony."* What emerged as a compromise instrument was the so-called Gunes Plan, named after Turkish Foreign Minister Turan Gunes, who occupied Ankara's bargaining seat at Geneva. (The Turks, in later disavowing the plan, called it the Kissinger Plan.) It made its first appearance at the conference table after the Greek Cypriots summarily rejected a proposal by Turkish-Cypriot representative Rauf Denktash that called for the reconstitution of Cyprus into two federated states with a geographical redistribution of population into each. The Gunes-Kissinger Plan created six new districts that would be operated by an autonomous Turkish-Cypriot administration covering 34 percent of the land area of the island, nearly twice as much as the Turkish share of the population. The largest of the Turkish enclaves under the scheme would be in the northern half—a triangle formed by the capital of Nicosia and the northern coastal resort cities of Kyrenia and Famagusta.

The Turkish proposals would have dismantled the original structure of the Cyprus republic by recognizing the existence of separate states with separate administrations—the very objective of Turkish policy for more than a decade. When Greek Foreign Minister George Mavros asked for a thirty-six-hour recess to consult with Athens, the Turks said no. They maintained afterward that the delay endangered the security of their troops in Cyprus. Callaghan angrily accused the Turks of having come to Geneva not to negotiate but simply to accept the capitulation of the Greeks.

Callaghan, at the urging of Washington, tried to keep the conference going while Kissinger sought to use his influence in Ankara to

---

Dispolitika (Foreign Policy). Cyprus, vol. 4, nos. 2 and 3. Ankara, Turkey: Foreign Policy Institute, 1974, pp. 46-65.

change the instructions of Gunes and allow the Greeks time to consider the proposal. According to one well-placed intelligence informant, Gunes placed a confidential call late Friday night to Ecevit in Ankara and said, in prearranged code, "My daughter is going on vacation." It was the signal for the opening up of the second offensive. The conference broke up well after midnight, and the general impression broadcast from Geneva was that the Turks had come in an inflexible mood with the second-stage invasion planned long in advance should they not get their way.

The outcome destroyed any illusion on Kissinger's part that he had a line of control through Ankara. Long-frustrated Turkish ambitions in Cyprus, the counterpart attitude of the Hellenic *enosis* movement, were now on the rampage. The Turks were wreaking their pent-up anger on city, countryside, and the Greek population of northern Cyprus. The Turks called it the continuation of their "peace operation." The Greeks called it Attila II.

On Saturday, August 13, the day the Gunes Plan was unveiled in Geneva and the eve of the collapse of the conference, Anderson announced that "the United States has been playing an active role in the negotiations" and that Kissinger "has been in frequent contact with Turkish Prime Minister Ecevit, including four times by telephone during the past twenty-four hours." For the first time in the public briefings on the crisis, the State Department also took a position on the merits of the Turkish claims in the dispute:

> The United States position is as follows: we recognize the position of the Turkish community on Cyprus requires considerable improvement and protection. We have supported a greater degree of autonomy for them. The parties are negotiating on one or more Turkish autonomous areas. The avenues of diplomacy have not been exhausted and therefore the United States would consider a resort to military action unjustified. We have made this clear to all parties.

Each word of the prepared statement had been gone over carefully by Kissinger and Sisco. It created shock waves of reaction in Greece and Cyprus, which were already in a state of outrage over the creeping advance of the Turkish forces during the cease-fire.

Yet, the public significance of the statement was never fully reported at the time. As a reinforcement to his private conversations with Ecevit, Kissinger was signaling publicly that the United States was coming down on Ankara's side of the dispute. The specific vehicle for achieving Turkey's objectives would be the Gunes Plan, which had been drawn up at Kissinger's request. Saturday, August 10, was the day that Washington got word through British intelligence that the Turks were marshaling for a second-stage offensive, thereby making moot any plan—American or otherwise—for a negotiated settlement.

Kissinger felt afterward that had he gone himself to Geneva in the critical phase of negotiations, the outcome would have been different. The Geneva conferences coincided, however, with the resignation of Richard Nixon, and Kissinger concluded that he should stay at the President's side. And so he spent the weekend in Washington, seeing ambassadors and assuring them that there would be no change in American foreign policy.

It was not long before the American embassies were being attacked by angry crowds in Athens and Nicosia. The statue of Truman in Athens was defaced and the doctrine that bore his name had never been in lower repute within Greece.

PART III

20. Congress Rebels: Battle of the Embargo

In the fall of 1974, Congress became the major battleground not only for the Cyprus dispute but for a number of major foreign policy controversies that had been brewing in the shadow of Vietnam.

For one thing, the American end game in Indochina was dragging on inconclusively despite Kissinger's declarations in October 1973 that "peace is at hand" in Vietnam. The continuing U.S. commitment to military support of the Thieu and Lon Nol regimes sustained as a cohesive opposition force the end-the-war coalition that transcended party and ideological lines. The Vietnam war was still the greatest obstacle to reestablishment of a national consensus in foreign policy, which had not been achieved since the early Kennedy years.

The souring of the public mood toward détente was also being expressed on Capitol Hill through rising criticism of normalization of trade relationships with the Soviet Union. This was most strikingly manifest in the broad and bipartisan coalition of anti-Soviet, pro-Israel, and civil libertarian support for the Jackson Amendment, named after its sponsor, Senator Henry Jackson (D-Washington), who was already being viewed as a major contender for the 1976 Democratic nomination. Jackson's amendment, co-sponsored in the House by Representative Charles Vanik (D-Ohio), was intended to maintain discriminatory trade and credit restrictions imposed during the Cold

War years on the Soviet Union and other Communist countries in reprisal for Soviet restrictions on emigration of Russian Jews to Israel.

There also arose in Congress a chorus of criticism of the $1.1 billion grain sale negotiated secretly by a consortium of American grain dealers with the Soviet Union with the knowledge and approval of President Nixon and his Secretary of State. Both the grain sale and the quadrupling of oil prices by the OPEC-industry cartels in the months after the October War became associated in public perception with the sharp increase during 1974 of prices in the grocery store and at the gasoline pump. The U.S. economy was sliding toward double-digit inflation and recession—stagflation—a condition that was already sapping the British and other West European economies.

What was unique about the oncoming domestic economic crisis of 1974 was that it seemed to be, in large measure, a product of foreign influences beyond the control of Washington and those who governed the American economy. And so it was only natural that the blame for the country's economic woes and the spreading sense of American economic impotence would be placed at the doorstep of those responsible for U.S. foreign policy.

Kissinger's initial zigzag course in dealing with the consequences of the OPEC price increases, from a tolerant stroking of the oil-producing shiekdoms to hints by the Nixon administration of military reprisal in the Persian Gulf, did nothing to enhance the confidence of the public or business community in his competence to deal with the challenge of the cartels. And so the mood, as the economic clouds darkened in the United States, was one of restiveness, distrust in foreign policy leadership, and rising public anger.

All this was set against the backdrop of Watergate and the impending collapse of the Nixon government. The shadow of the jailhouse lay heavily over the White House, paralyzing the upper levels of the executive branch and leaving Kissinger as one of the few functioning major figures in the debris of the Nixon administration.

Even Kissinger was becoming tarred with the scandal as a result of his controversial involvement in the "national security" wiretapping of seventeen government officials and newspapermen. Kissinger acknowledged his participation in the surveillance but disclaimed responsibility for it. His increasingly angry meetings with the press during June 1974 culminated in his explosive news conference in Salzburg, at which he threatened to resign unless he was vindicated by

Congress. The effect of Kissinger's jousts with the press, together with documentary evidence of his involvement in the wiretapping program turned up by the House Judiciary Committee's impeachment inquiry, aggravated the secretary's credibility problem in Congress.

There was still another background event that influenced congressional attitudes as the upheaval in Cyprus approached. It was the September 11, 1973, coup in Chile overthrowing the popularly elected coalition government of socialist Salvador Allende and imposing a military junta government that bore a striking resemblance to the colonels' regime in Greece. From the earliest days of the coup, there were strong indications of heavy American intervention in the downfall of the Allende government, which were later confirmed by the Senate Intelligence Committee. The committee revealed that President Nixon, with the knowledge and concurrence of Kissinger, ordered the CIA to support a coup against the Chilean President.

To the foreign policy liberals in Congress, the U.S. intervention in Chile, the intelligence revelations, the continuation of the war in Vietnam and Cambodia, as well as the U.S. relationship with the Greek junta were all of a piece. The common thread was Washington's embrace of totalitarian military regimes around the world as consistent with American security interests. It was becoming a widely circulated piece of Washington folk wisdom that Kissinger dealt most successfully with autocratic governments, whether in Athens, Moscow, or Hanoi, and least effectively with democracies.

When the tanks were unleashed against Archbishop Makarios by the Athens junta on the morning of July 15, 1974, there was a small body of congressmen who had critically watched the evolution of the colonels regime since it had seized power seven years earlier. The group included Representatives Don Edwards (D-California), Donald Fraser (D-Minnesota), John Brademas (D-Indiana), and Ben Rosenthal (D-New York) and Senators Claiborne Pell (D-Rhode Island), who was a friend of the ousted royal family, J. William Fulbright (D-Arkansas) and Vance Hartke (D-Indiana).

Two congressional staff members had for years proselytized the antijunta cause on Capitol Hill. They were James Pyrros of Representative Lucien N. Nedzi's office and Laverne Conway, who worked for Representative Edwards and was the wife of UAW official Jack Conway. Pyrros, of Greek descent, and Mrs. Conway, an ardent Hellenophile, were from Detroit and active in liberal Democratic politics, which centered about the Detroit chapter of Americans for Democratic Action, Solidarity House, and the UAW. They wrote speeches and encouraged statements of opposition to the junta, then made sure that the material was reprinted in the *Congressional Record* so that it could be picked up by the Greek press. Though the newspapers of Greece were heavily censored by the junta, they were permitted to reprint material from official sources such as the *Record*. By this ingenious arrangement, the *Congressional Record* became the political bulletin board and underground newspaper of the political opposition in Greece.

In 1971, Representative Rosenthal inherited the European Subcommittee of the House Foreign Affairs Committee and was persuaded to hold the first comprehensive public hearings on the events in Greece, thereby also providing a sounding board for the organized opposition to the regime. Exiled scholars, politicians, and journalists flocked to Washington to put on the public record their indictment of the colonels and their regime. The hearings provided a strong thrust to the antijunta cause and helped to solidify a bloc of congressional opposition to the Nixon-Kissinger policy of coexistence with the regime.

The junta was not, however, without its supporters in Congress. Among the most conspicuous boosters of the military government were Representatives Ed Derwinski and Roman Pucinski, both Chicago Democrats, as well as Greek-American legislators Peter Kyros (D-Maine) and Gus Yatron (D-Pennsylvania). Less than two weeks before the fall of the Ioannides government in July 1974, the regime presented decorations to Derwinski and Yatron during a visit by the two congressmen to Athens.

There was no immediate reaction on Capitol Hill to the Cyprus coup. The rush of events from the coup, to the remarkable escape of Makarios, to the Turkish invasion, to the crumbling of the junta in Athens and the disappearance of Nikos Sampson all came too quickly for political digestion. It was not until the second-stage Turkish "peace operation" in mid-August that the outline of a congressional response began to form.

On August 15, the day that Turkish forces were completing their mopping up of the northern half of Cyprus, a delegation of Greek-American congressmen, led by Brademas, trooped into the seventh-floor office of Secretary Kissinger after he granted their request for an audience.

Kissinger opened the meeting with the familiar touch of self-depre-cation with which he habitually tried to disarm his critics. The manage-ment of the Cyprus crisis at the State Department end, he conceded, had not been in the highest traditions of diplomacy. He reminded his visi-tors of his preoccupation with other state crises, not the least of them being the resignation of Nixon the previous weekend. But Kissinger was not beyond apportioning blame to the allies, and he unsparingly faulted British Foreign Secretary James Callaghan for mismanagement of the second Geneva conference on Cyprus, which had broken up in a shambles the previous evening.

As recounted by participants in the State Department meeting, Kissinger assured the visiting congressmen that the United States was by then engaged in "very active diplomacy" with the Turks and was insisting on assurances from Ankara that the troops would move no further. The only constructive events that had occurred in the Cyprus debacle, the secretary insisted, were the results of American pressure and initiative.

Brademas was the first to respond. "We are placing the blame squarely on you, sir," he was reported to have told the secretary. "We are not assigning responsibility for the failure of U.S. policy in Greece and Cyprus to President Ford. We feel it is yours."

The Indiana Democrat pronounced Kissinger's efforts at private diplomacy a failure. He asked why there had been no public protest from the State Department when Makarios was overthrown and nearly murdered, or when the Turks had invaded Cyprus. Why, he went on, were there no public statements of support for Callaghan in his efforts to keep the Turks from leaving the bargaining table in Geneva? Why was the State Department virtually silent during the ensuing military blitz by Turkish troops?

It was at this point that Brademas injected the proposal that the United States cut off its military assistance to Turkey until its troops were withdrawn from the island. This course of action was to become the subject of a year-long struggle between Congress and the executive branch.

Kissinger decried the congressional backlash on Cyprus as the prod-uct of a newly activated Greek lobby composed of Hellenic-American fraternal organizations, expatriate activists, and congressional agents, with the string pulled from the Foreign Ministry in Athens. He lashed out repeatedly in those days at the "Greek lobby" and "the Greek congressmen."

At the heart of Kissinger's annoyance was the congressional intrusion into the foreign policy process, an act that violated his view of the relationship between the executive and legislative functions. He further disdained those in Congress and the press who, in his view, were trying to cast the Cyprus matter as a "morality play."

From his own aerie of power and detachment, Kissinger looked down upon the East Mediterranean conflict not as a moral problem but as a challenge to "serious men engaged in serious purposes," as he was to say repeatedly to private audiences.

Brilliant as he was in the practice of private diplomacy and bureaucratic politics, Kissinger seriously misapprehended the temper of Congress on the Cyprus issue. He sought to deal through the traditional brokers of congressional consensus, the senior chairmen who held the established political franchises on Capitol Hill. But the 94th Congress, which convened in January 1975, included a class of seventy-five freshmen, a significant number of whom had matured politically on the war-torn campuses of the 1960s. There also had been changes in the congressional leadership brought about by reforms intended to break up the old power alignments that had governed Capitol Hill. The White House and Kissinger were slow to see the new political realities on Capitol Hill. By October 1974, when the administration was at the peak of its campaign to restore aid to Turkey, freshmen were being invited to the State Department en masse for audiences with the secretary and his principal deputies.

One of the persistent and underlying ingredients of the dispute between the secretary and his congressional opponents was the legality of continued American military assistance to Turkey after the occupation of northern Cyprus by Turkish troops.

The issue first arose at a press conference called by Kissinger on August 19, 1974, after the assassination of U.S. Ambassador to Cyprus Rodger P. Davies. James McCartney, diplomatic correspondent of the Knight newspapers, asked Kissinger whether the Foreign Assistance Act did not require the cutoff of American aid to Turkey as a result of its aggression in Cyprus.

"Well," Kissinger answered, "I will have to get a legal opinion on the subject, which I have not done."

He commissioned a study by his legal adviser, personal attorney, and friend, Carlyle J. Maw. Weeks and months passed and Kissinger steadfastly refused to disclose publicly the conclusions of the review.

Congressional and press inquiries brought the unvarying response that the study was "an internal working document."

The legal study became a major point of contention in the recurrent jousts between the press office and the news media. Five months after the State Department's legal opinion was completed, the department's spokesman Robert Anderson still found himself floundering with the issue.

"What is the justification," one reporter asked in a heated exchange in February 1975, "for keeping secret the results of a study that was ordered to determine whether or not a foreign government was in compliance with American law?"

"The study is not going to be made public," Anderson said. "The study was prepared at the secretary's request. He has discussed this entire subject—all the legal aspects, et cetera—with various committees of Congress. And I just can't take you any further."

During his confirmation hearings before the Senate Foreign Relations Committee in September 1973, Kissinger bound himself to the principle of compliance with the enactments of Congress. He did it in these words during an exchange with Senator Frank Church (D-Idaho):

> If what I have said to this Committee is to have any meaning, then it would be totally inappropriate for me as Secretary or as an advisor to the President to behave like a sharp lawyer and to try to split hairs and find some legal justification for something clearly against the intent of the law. So I think the better answer to you, Senator, is to say that when the law is clearly understood—and it will be my job to make sure that I clearly understand the intent of Congress—we may disagree with it, but once the intent is clear we will implement not only the letter but the spirit.

Almost a year after Kissinger uttered those words—on September 3, 1974—a State Department official came on a secret mission to the office of Senator Thomas Eagleton (D-Missouri). The official was deeply uneasy at having violated the code of the bureaucracy by going without authorization to a senatorial office. He met privately with Eagleton's chief foreign policy aide, Brian Atwood.

Never, he told Atwood, had he dreamed that he would be in the position he found himself. "This guy was stricken with a case of post-Watergate morality," recalled a witness to the meeting. "He said he could not understand why the highest level of government could still not obey the law."

The young official told Atwood that the legal study of the Turkish military aid question had been completed in the Office of the Legal Advisor. Its conclusion was that by no stretch of the statutes or the legal imagination of the State Department's attorneys could military aid to Turkey be continued. He said that pressure was being applied at the top of the department to modify the conclusions more to the tactical requirements of Kissinger by returning the unsatisfactory opinion to the staff for revision. The message, as read by Eagleton's staff, was that an attempt was being made to fiddle with the legal opinion and the State Department staff was holding firm to its position.

When Eagleton heard this account, he decided to plunge into battle on the issue of law and order—in this case, as it applied to the nation's foreign assistance programs. Two days after the anonymous State Department visit paid his office, Eagleton took the floor of the Senate. Without hinting of his special knowledge, the Missouri Democrat fired his first salvo of a debate in which he was to play a major role:

> We have just emerged from a trying period of American history—a period when laws were winked at and rationalized to fit the concepts of policymakers. By and large, we have learned that policies created in ignorance of or in spite of the law are doomed to failure.
> I am sure that it is not President Ford's intention to ignore the law in this instance. . . . But it is my belief that he is being ill advised *or being kept uninformed of the legal ramifications of his inaction in the Cyprus matter* in order to protect erroneous policy judgements made by the foreign affairs bureaucracy. (Emphasis added)

Eagleton refrained from attacking Kissinger by name. Frontal attacks on the secretary had not quite become fashionable in senatorial foreign policy debate. But the target of Eagleton's rhetoric was unmistakable.

On the morning of September 19, by a special arrangement with Senate Majority Leader Mike Mansfield (D-Montana), Kissinger was accorded permission to address the Senate Democratic caucus. It was a rare privilege for any outsider, let alone a cabinet officer in a Republican administration. Kissinger and the senators filed into room S-207, a hideaway off the Senate Chamber. The doors were closed and the press was barred. Kissinger hoped, by means of this extraordinary personal intervention, to make the case for rejection of a sense-of-Congress resolution by Eagleton with twenty-six co-sponsors to cut off military aid to Turkey.

The Eagleton resolution drew its argument from legal studies prepared by the Library of Congress and the General Accounting Office, both agencies of the legislative branch. It declared that continued U.S. military aid to Turkey was illegal under the laws governing the grant and sale of American weapons to other countries. It also proclaimed the sense of Congress to be that President Ford should declare Turkey immediately ineligible for further aid while its armed forces on Cyprus violated the terms for use of American arms. Since the resolution was not binding on the President, it could be read as a warning of more serious legislation ahead on the subject. Kissinger, at least, sensed that stronger congressional reaction was in the offing, and he considered it important that he nip the rebellion in the bud.

The Secretary of State was extraordinarily tense and humorless during the session. He began by urging the Democrats, as he put it, "not to write restrictions into the law that would tie President Gerald Ford's hands in dealing with the Cyprus issue."

At that point Eagleton rose and said, "We are not writing restrictions into the law, Mr. Secretary. All we ask is that you enforce the law on the books." He cited the conclusions of the two congressionally chartered reviews, which held that continued aid to Turkey was illegal.

Kissinger then confessed that he had received "a very complicated analysis from my legal people" and that "the dominant interpretation of my legal people is yours, Senator Eagleton." It was the secretary's first open confirmation that the suppressed State Department legal review supported the position of his opponents on the aid question.

"If my opinion is the dominant one and the right one, do you have any choice but to enforce it or seek its change by legislative   process?" Eagleton pressed.

"We are exploring our options and will consult with the appropriate Congressional leaders," the secretary responded.

"Do you have any alternative but to obey the law?" Eagleton persisted.

"Senator, if your legal opinion is correct, it will have very adverse foreign relations consequences for an important ally," Kissinger answered.

Mansfield, who had allied himself with the administration on the Turkish aid issue, had persuaded his Democratic colleagues to wait until Kissinger had been given a chance to make his case in the unusual forum of the caucus before voting on the resolution. But when the session adjourned and the members were back on the Senate floor, there were sixty-four votes for passage and twenty-seven against, with liberal Republicans deserting the administration's fold to vote with Eagleton.

Senator Adlai Stevenson (D-Illinois) may have expressed the consensus of the caucus on the Senate floor that day when he said, after hearing Kissinger:

> The U.S. failure in the past to perceive that morality and self-interest can coincide has already cost us the good will of the Greek people and the new Greek government. U.S. support for the Greek junta and disdain for the legitimate government of Cyprus are the proximate causes of the Cyprus coup, the Turkish invasion and now NATO's loss of Greece.
>
> Now, in order to repeat its mistakes of the past, the Administration seems prepared to violate the law.

This was the first significant skirmish in the Battle of the Cutoff, a political and legislative confrontation that was to continue for thirteen months before Congress partially turned on the tap of military assistance to Turkey. It generated a debate that embraced a full range of constitutional, moral, and national security arguments. Prior debates over the Nixon-Kissinger foreign policies had turned on specific issues —strategic arms policy, Soviet trade, Chile, Arab oil prices.

But the Cyprus dispute seemed to open the stoppers for broad philosophical attack by Kissinger's critics in Congress on the underlying assumptions of his policies and his methods. What was being challenged now was the strong executive dominance of the foreign policy process, which could now be identified with the two fiascoes of Vietnam and Watergate.

"The acid test of a policy . . . is its ability to obtain domestic support," Kissinger wrote in *A World Restored,* his study of post-Napoleonic Europe. His policies were now facing that test, not only in the East Mediterranean, but in the Middle East and Indochina, on his détente policy and balance-of-power diplomacy.

In October 1974, Congress twice passed and President Ford twice vetoed joint resolutions to ban military aid to Turkey until substantial progress was made toward a Cyprus settlement. Then President Ford agreed to a December 10 aid cutoff if there were still no movement. As negotiations foundered, the deadline was put back to February 5, 1975, by mutual White House-congressional agreement. Despite House and State Department efforts to further postpone the deadline and warnings that Turkey would close two dozen U.S. military and intelligence facilities there, Congress stuck to the February 5 date.

For Kissinger, Cyprus had advanced in priority from utter inconsequentiality prior to the coup to one of his biggest obsessions. It was not the diplomatic strategy of the conflict that seemed to absorb him so much as the political struggle with Congress. Kissinger pulled all the stops in his struggle to assert executive supremacy over the foreign policy process even though the policies of the executive branch placed it in violation of the law. The similarities with Watergate in the eyes of Eagleton and other opponents of the administration were chilling.

In Cyprus, there was now the specter of American weapons being used against each other by belligerent forces of two NATO allies on the soil of a friendly neutral state to whose continued sovereignty the United States was committed by international agreement.

Congress had adopted as a long-standing policy the principle that the United States should retain some form of control over its weapons exports, which during 1974 had reached an annual level of more than $10 billion.

India and Pakistan bloodied each other with American weapons in 1965 and the result was a temporary embargo on U.S. military aid to both countries. Again in 1971, a war broke out in the subcontinent fueled primarily by American equipment. In 1964 and 1967, Greece and Turkey came to the brink of full-scale conflict over Cyprus.

Senator John Pastore (D-Rhode Island) exclaimed at one point in the debate:

> The American people are a little fed up with taxpayers' money being used to feed bullets on both sides to people who are using these bullets to kill one another. I think the time has come when we have to put a stop to it. We went through this with Pakistan and India and had the same thing happen. All we are saying here is that, for the time being, what we ought to do is stop giving guns and bullets to people who are killing allies of the United States.

In 1964, when Turkey was on the verge of invading Cyprus in behalf of the beleaguered Turkish minority on the island, President Johnson admonished Turkish Prime Minister Inonu that under the bilateral agreements of 1947 between Washington and Ankara, "your government is required to obtain the United States' consent in the use of military assistance for purposes other than those for which such assistance was furnished. . . . I must tell you in all candor that the United

States cannot agree to the use of any United States supplied military equipment for a Turkish intervention in Cyprus under present circumstances."

Turkey sought to justify a military intervention on its role as a guarantor power under the London-Zurich Treaty of 1960, which was the charter of sovereign statehood for Cyprus. But Johnson scorned this argument. "I must call your attention," he wrote Inonu, "to our understanding that the proposed intervention by Turkey would be for the purpose of effecting a form of partition on the island, a solution which is specifically excluded by the Treaty of Guaranty."

In 1967, Johnson agreed to the partial arms embargo against the colonels' regime in Athens to signal American disapproval of the elimination by the Papadopoulos junta of constitutional government in Greece. Although, as described earlier, arms continued to flow into Greece under the "excess" weapons programs of the Pentagon in Washington, pressure grew more and more insistent within the Defense Department for full-scale restoration of aid to Greece. President Nixon lost little time in ending the symbolic embargo.

When Congress enacted the Foreign Assistance Act of 1961, it wrote a series of restraints into the program: Aid was earmarked for internal security, self-defense, participation in regional security arrangements, meeting requests for assistance by the United Nations and helping to "promote social and economic development" of the less developed "friendly" countries. The President was obliged to determine that those conditions had been met before authorizing or continuing to provide military aid. At the same time, he was required to declare a nation "immediately ineligible for further assistance" if it used American weapons in "substantial violation" of the Foreign Assistance Act restrictions.

Still another provision banned aid to "any country which the President determines is engaging in or prepjaring for aggressive military efforts directed against . . . any country receiving assistance under this or any other Act." Cyprus was the beneficiary of both foreign aid grants and support under the Food for Peace program.

But beyond the restrictions of the foreign aid statute books, there were additional restraints. The bilateral agreements signed between the United States and Turkey in 1947 and 1960 prohibited the diversion of American weapons to Cyprus or any other country without the prior consent of the President of the United States. This was the provision that President Johnson recited to Prime Minister Inonu.

The conclusion of the General Accounting Office report, which had been prepared at Eagleton's request, was that the use of U.S. military equipment in Cyprus placed Turkey in violation "as a matter of law" of the 1960 London-Zurich agreements, the 1947 bilateral agreements between Turkey and the United States, and the Foreign Assistance Act.

This was the heart of the legal case against continued American military aid to Turkey while its troops were deployed throughout the northern half of Cyprus. It was sufficiently compelling so that Kissinger never, in the course of the harshest conflict he experienced with Congress, chose to defend his policies on legal grounds.

Instead he argued executive prerogative. It was his responsibility as the President's chief international affairs adviser and not the prerogative of Congress to conceive and implement the broad lines of American foreign policy, as well as its day-to-day aspects.

Privately, at the dinner table with friends and admirers or in his informal klatches with sympathetic journalists, Kissinger accused Congress of having perpetrated a national disaster by interceding in the Cyprus dispute.

On January 25, 1975, in a speech to the Los Angeles World Affairs Council, which he entitled "Toward a New National Partnership," Kissinger sought to lay down the ground rules for a cooperative working relationship with Congress. The speech was preceded by all the fanfare accorded a major state document. A special press briefing was held in Washington just prior to delivery to make sure that the State Department regulars were aware of its gravity. The speech was reviewed for nearly a full week by Kissinger's top circle of advisers. Columnists were taken to lunch. Senior State Department officials were coached to stress in their contacts with the press the gravity with which Kissinger regarded his position on Capitol Hill.

In the speech, the secretary delivered a blunt entreaty to the lawmakers to refrain from intervening in the foreign policy process. "The growing tendency of Congress to legislate in detail the day-to-day or week-to-week conduct of our foreign affairs raises grave issues," the secretary warned. "American policy—given the wide range of our interests and responsibilities—must be a coherent and purposeful whole. . . . To single out individual countries for special legislative attention has unintended but inevitable consequences and risks unravelling the entire fabric of our foreign policy."

Kissinger then turned to the subject of military aid as a tool of foreign policy management. "If an important American interest is served by the aid relationship," he said, "it is a wise investment; if not, our resources are being squandered, even if we have no specific grievance against the recipient. For more and practical reasons, we must recognize that a challenge to the recipient's sovereignty tends to generate reactions that far transcend the merit of most of the issues in dispute."

In the case of the dispute over aid to Turkey, to which Kissinger was clearly referring, the transcendent issue for his critics in Congress remained the question of compliance with the law.

As the administration stepped up its campaign against the impending congressional embargo, President Ford appeared at a New York Republican fund-raising dinner and called for a return to the spirit of the late Arthur Vandenberg. Vandenberg had viewed Congress and the Senate Foreign Relations Committee he headed as a handmaiden of the presidency on foreign policy matters, a viewpoint expressed in his aphorism, "Politics stops at the water's edge."

Eagleton, in a Senate speech of February 12, 1975, sought to answer both the Kissinger and Ford appeals for congressional compliance as well as their defenders in the media. He said:

> We must realize that there is no turning the clock back to the institutional relationships of the Cold War era. That period was characterized by a clear understanding of common goals, the acceptance of a common enemy, and the total subordination, largely self-imposed, of the Legislative Branch. . . . The most grievous errors of American policy in the past decade can be traced to a decision-making process which has not benefited from institutional balance.
>
> The American people were too often presented with *faits accomplis* in foreign policy because Congress was unaware of the important commitments being undertaken by the Executive Branch. From Vietnam to the India-Pakistan dispute, to Chile, to our current Cyprus policy, initiatives were taken in the name of the American people without the advice and consent of their elected representatives in Congress.

Kissinger had paid tribute in his Los Angeles speech to the "indispensable contribution of Congress to the general direction of national policy." But Eagleton acidly noted that "when 'national policy' was set by statute in the case of our military assistance laws . . . the law was circumvented to accommodate an attitude that there exists a higher order of interest."

The harshest outcry against Kissinger was delivered by Senator Adlai Stevenson on February 12, 1975:

"Now that history has stripped the policies of Henry Kissinger of their pretensions to grandeur and his actions of their pretensions of success, the Secretary is casting the blame upon the Congress," Stevenson declaimed.

Congress, he said, was being blamed for Soviet repudiation of the 1973 trade bill, for the fiasco in Cyprus, for the then-impending fall of the Thieu and Lon Nol regimes in Indochina. He went on:

> The Congress is to blame for the deterioration of America's position in the world, but not for the reasons assigned by the Secretary of State. Congress is to blame because for too long its members naively applauded the adventures of Henry Kissinger and Richard Nixon. Unwittingly, they became part of the personality cult, charmed at dinner parties, dazzled by the disingenuous intellect. . . . Now in the twilight they see the errors of personal diplomacy and the danger of liaisons with rotting and totalitarian regimes the world over.

Kissinger accepted the growing attacks on his foreign policy leadership with an attitude of philosophical detachment. He communed with friendly columnists.

Joseph Alsop, a confidant and loyal defender of Kissinger, wrote in the *Washington Post* of January 27, 1975, of the secretary's pessimism over the "long-term power of survival of the American society that he now serves so well." Kissinger, Alsop wrote, is "worried about what has been happening in American 'establishment,' the increasing weakness of vital American institutions, the difficulty of governing America in its present mood and state—all these are constantly repeated concerns of the Secretary of State."

To another journalist friend, *New York Times* columnist James Reston, Kissinger said of the mounting criticism of his policies: "I would think what has happened now after President Nixon's resignation is the opening of foreign policy to normal partisan debate. Probably in the excitement, the pendulum is swinging a bit too far."

Despite the increasingly critical clamor, the secretary pursued his attempts at private diplomacy in Athens and Ankara while in Washington he keyed his campaign to the politics of national security.

Under Kissinger's direction, a team of administration officials and congressional allies painted dire scenarios in the East Mediterranean.

One was that unless aid were restored, Turkey would pull out of military participation in NATO, following the lead of Greece in July 1974. And there was also the specter of the Turks realigning their foreign policy eastward toward the Soviet Union or the Arab world.

Senate Majority Leader Mansfield, who was firmly allied with the administration on the issue of the Turkish embargo, recited that prospect to his colleagues in a speech. He said:

> If we adopt an amendment aimed directly and specifically against Turkey, what might be the result? For one thing, we might see a tilt on the part of Turkey toward the Soviet Union. They have a thousand-mile frontier, and within that area they have nuclear warheads and U.S. installations—our warheads and our installations. Up to now, Turkey has maintained a hands-off attitude as far as the Middle East is concerned. But the Turks are a Moslem people. Perhaps there might be a tilt on the part of Turkey toward what we call the Middle East. Perhaps that will have a decided effect, too.

Mansfield's arguments raised few flutters of concern among his colleagues. Turkey and Russia had been divided by centuries of conflict. Kissinger had himself written about the implacable hostility of Tsar Alexander to the Ottoman rulers in the nineteenth century. Also, the Turks had conspicuously cast their lot with their Moslem brethren as recently as the 1967 and 1973 Arab-Israeli wars by denying their ally, the United States, landing rights for support flights to the Israelis.

Two weeks before the embargo was due to go into effect, the Turkish government intensified its own pressures on Congress by announcing that it would impose sanctions against the American bases if the aid ban were enacted. On January 31, State Department spokesman Anderson proclaimed that the congressional aid deadline was undermining the prospects for a settlement in Cyprus "because it puts pressure on one of the parties" and could well drive Turkey from the Western alliance. On February 4, the day before the embargo was due to take effect, the Turkish government declared ominously that the cutoff would require it to review the entire balance sheet of its NATO obligations and its bilateral defense arrangements with the United States.

But the administration's national security trump cards were the electronic monitoring facilities aimed at the Soviet Union from secret installations at Sinop, Diyarbakir, and Karamursel operated by the National Security Agency.

The American intelligence community depended upon the three monitoring sites for valuable information on a wide variety of Soviet military activities. The sophisticated electronic ears at the stations spied on Soviet ABM launches, military communications, troop movements, advance research and development, and also were intended to serve as an early-warning line in the event of a nuclear warhead launch by the Russians. At background briefings, select congressmen and members of the press were told of the crucial role played by the sites in detecting the forward movement of Soviet airborne units during the 1973 Middle East War.

Time magazine was able to report early in August that the highly sophisticated electronic equipment in the U.S. sites had performed "prodigious feats" of intelligence that included the detection of nuclear warheads aboard Soviet freighters bound for Syria and Egypt during the 1973 Middle East War.

Kissinger, by virtue of his multiple role as arbiter of national security matters, supplier and consumer of intelligence, architect of policy, and custodian of secrets, was able to define the threat while at the same time guarding access to the body of classified information by which his case could be tested. It gave him a formidable advantage in the debate with Congress. Rarely could he be tripped up by qualified experts outside the governmental security system he controlled.

In one case, this did happen. The administration had been contending that among the functions performed by the Turkish installations was the monitoring of Soviet ICBM launches to determine whether they were in compliance with the Strategic Arms Limitation Talks (SALT). In fact, Fred Ikle, Director of the U.S. Arms Control and Disarmament Agency, claimed that closure of the Turkish bases could limit the American ability to monitor Soviet compliance with the SALT I agreement. But this was publicly questioned by former CIA Deputy Director for Science and Technology Herbert Scoville, who said that the monitoring stations in Turkey were not properly positioned for such a role. To monitor the Soviet launches, he said, the sites would have to be some 2,000 miles to the east, in Iran. Afterward, CIA Director William E. Colby acknowledged to a House committee that the Turkish sites had no significant role in the SALT I monitoring network. The administration subsequently dropped this argument.

When Clifford went to Ankara during his February, 1977 trip, he neglected to mention U.S. concern over the closed intelligence facilities during the first, then the second, and then the third day of his consultations. Finally one of the Turkish conferees asked, with a show of impatience, whether Clifford did not want to talk about the intelligence stations which had been a major concern to the preceding administration in Washington.

"Oh, the intelligence stations," Clifford is reported to have responded with lawyerly coolness. "No, we're not too concerned. We've made other arrangements."

It was an approach in marked contrast to the noisy alarms of Kissinger whose policies had made the intelligence bases political hostages to Turkish intentions.

But there was no dispute that the monitoring stations together with the conventional military and air installations and atomic weapons storage sites in Turkey weighed heavily in U.S. military and NATO consideration. In a military context, the monitoring stations were equally useful to Turkey, and it is significant that when the Turks finally did make good on their threat to close down the intelligence facilities, they left open the joint military installations of greatest local benefit.

Nonetheless, the embargo went into effect on February 5, shutting off the pipeline of grants, credits, and commercial military sales to Turkey, including aircraft deliveries that had already been paid for by the Turkish government. Although President Ford had discretionary power to grant $50 million a year in assistance to the Turks, the administration declined to tap this emergency authorization with the private explanation that the Turkish government considered this an insulting political palliative. The paramount Turkish concern at this point was its ability to maintain parity, if not superiority, with the Greeks in air power. When the embargo was imposed, Turkey was engaged in a major modernization of its air forces through the purchase of F-104 and F-4 fighters to match the high-performance jet fighter acquisitions of the Greeks, all under the U.S. assistance programs to meet the supposed requirements of NATO. Fundamentally, what had happened was that Turkey had been dealt out of its arms race with Greece by the chief supplier of weapons to both countries as a result of the congressional embargo.

During the eight months of the embargo, the administration tried to tighten the ratchets of political pressure on Congress to reverse itself to mollify the Turks. Turkish Foreign Minister Sabri Caglayngil announced on June 17 that all U.S. military and intelligence-gathering facilities in Turkey would be placed on "provisional status." The next week, President Ford met personally with Brademas and other key House members on three separate occasions in an effort to persuade them to relax the embargo. The State Department also lobbied briskly on Capitol Hill, and freshmen House members found themselves being invited to backgrounders with Kissinger and his principal deputies, Assistant Secretaries Arthur Hartman, Robert McCloskey, and, when available, U.S. Ambassadors to Turkey and Greece William Macomber and Jack Kubic.

Nonetheless, on July 31, 1975, the House refused by one vote to end the embargo. The scales of congressional opinion on the embargo issue were exceedingly close. Two months earlier, the Senate had agreed—also by one vote—to lift the embargo.

Ankara, in response to the congressional action, dropped the other shoe and closed down the intelligence stations in August. Though the power was cut off at the facilities, the U.S. personnel were permitted to remain in place in anticipation of their reopening.

Nothing of significance happened, however, to ameliorate the deepening impasse on Cyprus. Indeed, Cyprus was all but forgotten in a new international crisis that centered on Turkey's importance in the priority of U.S. security interests. Under the cover of military occupation, Turkey was effecting a de facto annexation of the northern sector of the island. Turkish-Cypriot refugees were recirculated from the south through Turkey into northern Cyprus, where they occupied the homes and farms abandoned by the fleeing Greek-Cypriot refugees. The partition of Cyprus, which Makarios had staved off for fourteen years, though risking two full-scale wars in the East Mediterranean, had now become a fact—the "new reality," which Turkish-Cypriot leader Rauf Denktash proclaimed behind the shield of 35,000 Turkish troops.

For seven months after the Turkish occupation, U.S. arms flowed freely to Ankara and there was no progress on Cyprus. For the next eight months, American military aid to Turkey was banned and there was still no progress. The deadlock persisted to the end of the Ford presidency, despite endless rounds of meetings between all parties to the dispute.

In the closing months of Ford's term, Kissinger, his maneuvering time running out, was still counting on the sweet carrot of military aid to cajole concessions from Turkey. On March 26, 1976, President

Ford signed a new defense treaty with Turkey and appealed to Congress for its speedy passage. It called for a program of $1 billion in new military aid over a four-year period and also provided for reopening the U.S. intelligence stations closed down by Turkey after the 1975 arms embargo was adopted. At the time the Turkish treaty was signed, a companion aid program for Greece was being negotiated in the bureaucracy to provide $700 million over the same four-year period in exchange for renewal of the U.S. leases on its Greek bases.

The outgoing Ford administration assigned top legislative priority to the Turkish military deal, deploying on Congress the combined persuasive talents of Kissinger, the State Department's top diplomatic team, and NATO officials. Congressional opponents of the Ford-Kissinger approach who were more sympathetic to the Greek position —and this included the Senate's most influential Democrats—insisted on delay, at least until the two defense treaties for Greece and Turkey could receive simultaneous consideration by Congress.

And this was the posture of things when time ran out on Gerald Ford and Henry Kissinger.

The Greeks in Athens and Nicosia had placed their bets on a new Democratic administration in Washington. When Jimmy Carter was elected President, a school holiday was declared in Cyprus, and when his emissary, Clark Clifford, arrived in Athens in February, there were crowds and cheers such as no American official had received in years. Conversely, the Clifford mission received, at least initially, a cool reception in Ankara. The Turks had come to regard Kissinger as their friend in the otherwise hostile court of American public opinion.

But the Carter administration came to the triangular quagmire of the Greek-Turkish-Cyprus dispute with inherited assumptions and policies: the primacy of maintaining the NATO military alliance with appropriate force levels, the need to avoid conflict between Greece and Turkey on the Mediterranean flank, the encouragement of U.S. political orders friendly to the status quo in Greece, Turkey and Cyprus. In this framework, the problems of Cyprus are secondary, despite the tens of thousands of Greek Cypriots turned into refugees, the vast expropriation by the Turkish occupation force of Greek-Cypriot homes and businesses, and the division of the island into two strictly divided sectors for the separate populations. In NATO terms, the nonaligned state of Cyprus is, as Clifford put it, "a constant exacerbation in the East Mediterranean."

The first initiatives of President Carter and Secretary of State Vance were to raise the military ante for Turkey, increasing the annual ceiling for arms sales from the Ford-Kissinger limit of $125 million to $175 million in fiscal 1978. In addition, Vance proposed to Congress additional authorization to permit Turkey's purchase of forty new F-4 jet fighters with which Turkey hopes to maintain parity with Greece in airpower, though Turkey holds an immense advantage in land forces.

Clifford was able to persuade the four sides to the dispute to convene a meeting in Vienna during the first week of April 1977, at which the Greek and Turkish Cypriots presented their alternate approaches to settle the division of territory and government power on the island.

The two sides had often shown readiness to talk though rarely to agree, and Vienna was yet another meeting at which they stood apart: the Turkish Cypriots this time unwilling to consider new territorial proposals which the Greek Cypriot negotiators made as part of an initiative by Clifford to get negotiations moving again.

The death of Makarios on August 3, 1977—almost on the third anniversary of the military annexation by Turkish troops of the northern third of Cyprus—removed from the scene the one truly national leader of the Greek Cypriot people with the authority to speak for all of them. Those in the State Department and the foreign ministries of other countries who regarded Makarios as the largest obstacle to a settlement would now have the opportunity to see their thesis tested. On the other hand, the disappearance of Makarios from the political stage could well have inaugurated a period of political chaos on the island that would raise the level of danger.

In Turkey, as well, events took an ominous turn with the restoration to power of the conservative coalition under Demirel two days prior to the death of Makarios. There had been hopes in Washington and other western capitals that the general election the previous June would provide a clear mandate to the liberal and western-oriented Social Democrat, Bulent Ecevit, with which to negotiate a Cyprus settlement. But Ecevit failed to win a vote of parliamentary confidence. The floundering Demirel coalition of hard-line nationalistic and pro-Islamic parties was little disposed toward a conciliatory line on Cyprus. Afflicted as it was with deepening economic conditions at home and a disastrous foreign exchange deficit the Turkish government might be tempted, as was the Greek military regime only a few years earlier, to use Cyprus and the Aegean disputes to draw attention from domestic adversities.

Epilogue

Today the Aegean and East Mediterranean are, more than ever, seas of tension. Nationalistic and political conflict continue to hover close to the point of explosion. It is a region in which the policies of the Cold War, inaugurated during the second Truman administration, have survived in purest form the politics of summitry and the diplomacy of détente. Greece and Turkey have been consecrated under petrified military doctrines of NATO to an alliance that fails to recognize their histories, their politics, and their separate national ambitions.

Since the United States has chosen to play such an influence in the post-World War II evolution of Turkey and Greece, it is not inappropriate to view the present state of affairs as the product, in large measure, of flawed American foreign policy. In Greece and Turkey, the United States is no longer regarded as a guarantor of survival as it was in the golden days of reconstruction immediately after World War II.

In Greece, the United States had become widely perceived as the mainstay of the military dictatorship that brutalized the country's constitutional system for eight years and a co-conspirator in the coup against Archbishop Makarios and the subsequent Turkish partition of Cyprus. In Turkey, the humiliation of the military aid cutoff by Congress rankles as deeply as President Johnson's 1964 ultimatum to Ankara against intervening in behalf of the Turkish-Cypriot minority.

In Cyprus, there is almost universal suspicion of a Kissinger tilt toward Turkey through devious and complex political manipulation that can be conceived only by the Byzantine imagination—even in the absence of concrete evidence to support it.

The underlying policy of Washington toward the East Mediterranean has been to foster an arms race in both countries in the name of common NATO goals. It was inevitable that the billions of dollars in armaments poured into the two Aegean powers would distort their internal political development. The effect was to enhance the authority of the conservative, military-backed parties and leaders who were willing to serve as instruments of those policies. The Greek dictatorship was seen by most of its opponents as an almost inevitable consequence of both the massive and continuing U.S. investment in the military sector of Greek society and Washington's open disapproval of the civilian leaders who stressed economic reform and development as well as disengagement from Cold War entanglements.

While the United States has professed a public policy of support for democratic and constitutional principles, the unarticulated thrust of its influence has been to align itself with the politics of status quo. This is reflected in the panicked reactions of Henry Kissinger to the leftward political currents along the Mediterranean tier of countries from Portugal to Greece. Kissinger's denunciations of the European Communist parties were strikingly reminiscent of the attacks by Metternich and Castlereagh, those two great practitioners of early nineteenth century "cabinet diplomacy," on the comparable European movements in their era.

In *A World Restored*, Kissinger described the unlimited diplomatic charter enjoyed by the two men, Castlereagh of Britain and Metternich of Austro-Hungary, who were untrammeled by parliament or bureaucracy. They too sought to apply balance-of-power diplomacy toward the creation of a stable association of nation-states to secure Europe against the liberal and revolutionary currents then stirring in the embers of the Napoleonic order.

Kissinger's description of their joint maneuvering against the Greek independence insurrection of 1821, the liberal and romantic revolution of the day, is remarkably pertinent to the events in the East Mediterranean 153 years later.

The Greek national liberation struggle against its Ottoman rulers inspired sympathy throughout Europe, from so diverse a cast of fig-

ures as the poet Byron and Tsar Alexander. In cruel reprisal against
the insurrection, the Turks were slaughtering Greeks and hanging
their bishops in the door of the Greek Orthodox Primate's cathedral
at Constantinople.

Tsar Alexander, who was outraged by the Turkish barbarities and
who considered himself the protector of the Greek-Orthodox faith,
was champing to intervene in behalf of the Greeks. But Castlereagh
and Metternich saw the Greek insurrection and the prospect of a Russian attack on the Ottomans as a threat to the balance of power they
had sought to restore in post-Napoleonic Europe.

Kissinger described Castlereagh's disingenuous approach to the
Tsar, urging the Tsar in a letter not to intervene in behalf of the in-
surrectionaries. "Castlereagh," wrote Kissinger, "did not deny that
the atrocities committed by the Turks 'made humanity shudder.' But,
like Metternich, he insisted that humanitarian considerations were
subordinate to maintaining 'the consecrated structures of Europe
which would be jarred to the core by any radical innovation.' " The
similarity to the circumstances in the East Mediterranean after the
July 1974 coup is striking.

Viewed in contemporary geopolitical terms, Turkey, was, like the
Ottoman Empire, a barrier to expanding Russian influence in the East
Mediterranean. Modern spying technology gave it additional importance as a U.S. national security asset, a valuable listening post on
the Russian flank. Its proficient standing army of 450,000 and the
strong influence of the military in Turkish society weighed strongly
with the national security establishment in Washington.

Greece, once it broke the grip of the colonels' rule, had again become a political question mark. As the political party system was
again enfranchised, the exiles returned and the mandate of popular
opinion once more became relevant to the conduct of the nation's
affairs. For Karamanlis, in the 1950s a conservative pillar of the Western alliance, the price of political survival in 1974 was withdrawal
from military participation in NATO. The certitudes of the dictatorship, at least in the Papadopoulos period, were replaced by the risks
of democratic process.

Cyprus, with the survival and return—until his death in 1977—of
the independent-minded Makarios, was perceived by Kissinger as it
was by Ball and Acheson and later by Clifford as a persistent threat to
the stability of the NATO alliance. It is for this reason that the division

of the island into regions of Turkish and Greek influence has had a permanent allure to Washington decisionmakers.

But Kissinger misjudged the stubbornness of Makarios, the territorial ambitions of Turkey, the political volatility of Greece, and the adversary temper of Congress.

The history of American diplomacy in the East Mediterranean has not been wholly monochromatic, a pure example of Cold War doctrine working its power over events. This history, as I have tried to show, was etched by statesmen and bureaucrats of varying quality operating under direction from Washington which reflected, from time to time, attitudes of apathy and ambiguity as well as interventionism.

But there were certain dominant biases in American policy rooted in the Cold War assumptions of the late 1940s which, more often than not, aligned the influence of the United States against those parties and leaders advocating popularly based reform programs and toward the status quo politics of the palace, the military general staff, and the political establishment.

In the case of Greece and Turkey the military relationships conceived in the name of NATO became the driving imperatives of foreign policy, with powerful blandishments of money and weaponry, rather than a component of a policy in which social and humanitarian considerations were given serious weight.

Toward Cyprus the American attitude was schizophrenic, with its public professions of support for the elected government headed by Makarios and its tacit support for policies and political forces seeking to assimilate Cyprus into the dominion of NATO by means of partition.

Even after the 1974 coup there was a clear consensus within the upper levels of the Department of State against the return of Makarios to Cyprus during the 1974 post-crisis negotiations. This feeling was epitomized in Kissinger's previously recounted comment that Archbishop Makarios was "too big a man for so small an island."

In Kissinger's view Cyprus must have appeared as a gnat in his vision of an American foreign policy restored from its ten-year obsession with Vietnam, perhaps in the same way that the Greek insurrection of 1821 appeared to Metternich as a poignant but inconsequential episode in the path of his efforts to reconstitute the European balance of power.

Metternich's diplomacy was erected upon the closed and well-ordered political universe of the Holy Alliance. Kissinger's diplomacy was constructed at one political level on the scaffolding of the post-

World War II anti-Communist alliances. Metternich played on the conflicts between Russia and the Ottoman rulers. Kissinger fashioned his policy of détente on the conflicts between Moscow and Peking, fundamental divisions of national interest which long pre-dated their divisions over Marxist-Leninist doctrine.

But neither Metternich nor Kissinger nor the Cold War architects made room in their policies for the politics of change and redistribution that were at work in their respective eras.

And so while Kissinger's contribution was to purge American foreign policy of the Protestant missionary spirit with which Dulles had imbued it, his failure was in not understanding the imperatives of change among and within nations: toward government by popular consensus, toward reducing the disparities of wealth and ·poverty, toward the processes of both reform and revolution. An American foreign policy that fails to comprehend these forces may be doomed to sterility and failure.

Author's Note

In many more cases than I would have wished, I was obliged to honor the ground rule of nonattribution requested by U.S. and foreign officials who felt it would have been impossible for them to speak freely on any other terms. Many of the interviews conducted with American policymakers came at a time when strong restraints were in force within the State Department on discussion of matters pertaining to the events of this book. These inhibitions were also felt by members of the foreign diplomatic community who were concerned that any attributed remarks could well be prejudicial to the interests of their governments in Washington. The Department of State refused to declassify material I requested under the Freedom of Information Act on grounds that their release "could damage the conduct of our foreign relations." An appeal of my request filed by Mark Lynch, attorney for the Center for Responsive Law, was rejected by John E. Reinhardt, then Assistant Secretary of State for Public Affairs and now director of the United States Information Agency.

Index